Mere Animals

Thomas Spriggs

ISBN: 9781793318107

DEDICATION

To all those resisting the Leftist mob.

CONTENTS

Acknowledgments   i

Forward   1

Part One: Twilight

1   The Animal Farm   4

2   A Star Wars Future   12

3   Where Nothing Leads   31

4   The Truth About Twilight   59

5   The God of Sometimes   67

Part two: To Be mere Animals

6   Death by Hubris   80

7   The Blind Leading the Blind   97

8   The Value of Nothing   106

9   The Great God Rome   116

10   Lying Liars Who Lie All The Time   125

Response

11	The Struggle	132
12	How to be Change	139
13	The Reign of Peace	144
14	Some Final Words	150

ACKNOWLEDGMENTS

I wish to thank God for inspiration and protection. He provided so much of what I needed to be able to work on this book unencumbered and without distraction without my input. To Him be the glory. Also to my family, who have always given me space to be myself.

FORWARD

Growing up, one of my biggest influences was *Mere Christianity* by C.S. Lewis. His clear thinking and analysis of the nature of Christian belief solidified my own belief in God, and caused my faith to grow over time. I am completely indebted to the man, and in heaven today he can point to me as one of the jewels of his ministry.

It was a long and tortuous road that brought me to where I am today. Over the decades my faith waxed and waned as I married and divorced, became a father, pursued an education and restarted my life. As I have grown, I have come to understand the theological rock of Mr. Lewis better than ever before.

So it is no accident I chose the title of this book based on his. Today, we have a virulent and evangelical New Atheism that does not just deny faith but mocks it. And we are facing a new Hard Left that bases its identity on struggling against the ideals and values of western civilization. They insist we really are merely intelligent animals, a not so happy accident of nature, and embrace all the philosophical ideas that comes with that.

The most modern version of the communist philosophy of struggle is the corrosive belief in postmodernism, that all of politics and economics are a struggle for power. Original Marxist belief was that the middle and upper classes (the bourgeoisie) were the oppressors of the lower classes. When it turned out the middle classes of various countries were not turned on by being labeled the enemy, communism morphed into postmodernism in the West and anti-colonialism in Africa.

As the Soviet Union slowly collapsed from the 1970's to the 1990's the new theology of postmodernism lacked popular support. The corrupt communist system was so clearly inferior to the capitalist system there was no way to hide it. The fall was spectacular, a slow-motion train wreck that had all the drama and fireworks of the best television series.

Now, enough time has passed to allow for the rise of postmodernism through a new generation that did not know the Soviet god of their professors. They are much easier to convince of the supposed evils of the victorious capitalists. Growing up in a time of political and economic instability, the Youth of America have become an easy mark.

Yet there is a disconnect here; despite the consistent and increasing numbers of terrorist attacks by Muslim supremacists, they have all but ignored the real threat Islam presents to the future of the world. Instead they focus on imaginary enemies who to a large majority do not exist. Institutional racism, the patriarchy, and Christian theocracists haunt the empty halls of the imagination of the Hard Left in the West.

Along with the new Hard Left, a New Atheist

movement has blossomed among the young in a way it never had before. Lacking comprehension, the young have somehow been convinced that terrorist attacks committed by Islamic supremacists are the fault of Christians who neither supported nor committed the atrocities. Modern life and communications have short-circuited the logic board of the average youth.

Just as C.S. Lewis made plain the ideals and inner and outer life of Christianity, this book will attempt to provide a picture of the understandings and consequences of the rise of postmodernism. These consequences will be held up to the reality of expansionist Islam, and how postmodern thought will slowly cripple our ability to defend ourselves, first from their ravages then later from their dominance.

PART ONE: TWILIGHT

CHAPTER ONE
THE ANIMAL FARM

It is insidious, our tendency to ruin gardens. We humans have done it from the beginning, when Adam and Eve were still in *The* Garden, this ruining of hope. We cannot help ourselves. Like a moth to the flame, civilization has imploded upon itself over and over, to be replaced by the next tribe up. One after another, great empires have risen, faltered, and crashed back down. Never satisfied, we have garnered destruction to our breast as like an only son.

We were born for the garden, made to be able to use it's ability to provide in powerful and fantastical ways. What else would you call an iPad? Where do you think the materials for your iPad came from? From our garden, this miraculous place where we are lucky enough to live. From our minds, where compared to other animals we share the planet, with which we have godlike intelligence.

Still we have a love/hate relationship with the garden.

We fawn over it, rejoice in it, yet have a deep-seated desire to smother it in the cradle. We curse the garden even as we eat of the fruit it so graciously supplies. Made from it's very dirt in our physical bodies we nevertheless assert our independence of it through our intellect. We curse our own biology while wiping out smallpox and polio.

None of this makes sense, unless you remember the fall, the time when we were removed from The Garden and placed in our current damaged version. But it is not just that the garden is imperfect; we ourselves were damaged in our uprooting in ways both ocular and concealed. Worse, we have been mis-wired in such a way we cannot easily see our own psychic twisting. Even I fall under it's spell, and I am self-aware enough to know better.

Mankind is a self-deluding species. From cradle to grave, the vast majority of people are have far, far, far too much "self-esteem" and far, far, far too little humility. Ours is the age of the White Knights, where everyone rides across the internet saving the world from whatever evil they have determined besmirches it. Nearly everyone approaches social media as if they are already famous celebrities and clearly unmatched geniuses, when in truth they are no such thing. Every lemming sees himself a king.

We overestimate practically everything, and nothing like our own contributions. We pretend civilization is this shiny, stainless steel orb of perfection, or at least could be. We ignore the fact that civilization was built through a long, slow, painful and bloody slog. We exaggerate our own contributions, despite the fact that the majority of those who are important in business and science worked long hard hours to get there, and the rest of us don't matter all that much in comparison.

But we misunderestimate nothing like our level of understanding of the universe. Most everyday humans are absolutely convinced of their social clarity and rightness of thought. We see ourselves as having walked out of the cave of Plato and into the light of unlimited knowledge. We really believe, for the most part, that we have cracked open the fount of all wisdom. We scoff at religion, tradition, and wisdom. We have the Hubble telescope, after all. Our stock brokers are all we really need.

The truth is more mundane. We are in fact nowhere near the godlike beings we imagine and ourselves as (and pretend to be on social media). Yes, we have made impressive scientific advancements, especially since the Industrial Revolution, but we regularly draw wrong conclusions about much of the universe and even our own nature. For most people most of the time, ego inflation has been a minor nuisance. That is changing as we throw off the shackles of humility in our modern society.

Today, we face the challenge of a new Hard Left, centered around an upstart movement of New Atheism. Atheism was always a small movement in the world, and a minor part of the American public. Now, it's numbers are growing, fed by writers such as Sam Harris and Richard Dawkins. What was once a small percentage of Americans has now become a sizable force.

According to them, we are merely animals, nothing more that intelligent monkeys (yet nearly all-powerful). God is an outdated and facile idea. Believers are weak, degenerate, and illogical. People of faith live off emotions over understanding. They even deny science!

The New Atheists are obviously superior in every way, especially when if comes to understanding and supporting science. It is their core belief that all human problems are solvable, if technology is correctly applied to the situation(s). Eventually, technology will give us wings and set us free to explore the stars and break us free from the divisions that separate us.

One day, we will all be able to live on a star ship, flitting about the galaxy and making wondrous discoveries about the other life in the universe (assuming there is any). The Hard Left sees itself as reaching for the stars with it's feet firmly planted on the ground. It is certainly a beautiful dream.

But it may not be so easy to make it so. We can barely make it to the moon in person, and then only through incredible effort. We have sent hardly enough probes everywhere else in the universe to be but a smattering of inquisition and knowledge. We are even now constantly caught off guard by what we observe through the scientific process. Humans know almost nothing about the planet we live on much less the rest of it.

Most importantly, this vision of the Star Trek future is itself a divorcement from reality. It does not reflect the reality of human nature. Development from childhood to adulthood is a perilous and tenuous journey, and the constant low levels of violence found universally and in the most peaceful societies worldwide belie the truth of human nature. There is no evidence technology can actually change human nature, in particular the more limiting parts of the soul.

The most important flaw in the future described by the Hard Left is that humans are fungible; that our response to existence itself can be intentionally mentally adjusted through interaction with technology. We do not have a single example of this in the way they mean it, but as I will explain later the New Atheism places the future of the entire human race on this assumption. This error leads to another, that we are struggling through today, the belief that all people should be treated exactly the same.

Belief in absolute equality is a direct example of projection. The Hard Left makes the jump from the future in which humans are conformed by technology to pretending and proclaiming that is how the bulk people are now, a complete and utter fallacy. Life and death issues in the world hang on whether we are going to continue to play pretend this way with bad people. Plato would be saddened.

He would point out we are clearly still in the cave, having done nothing more than added a few sticks to the fire that illuminates the world. It is difficult to know the difference between twilight and dawn even after all our effort, and the separation of them is actually so sparse in the cave. It takes only a few short years for the industrious to lead the majority astray in terrible and bloody ways. We have powerful examples; the Communists of the 1920's and the Nazi's of the 30's.

According to the New Atheism we are literally Animal Farm, and beyond knowledge there is little value in wisdom or beauty. Just as in the original story, some animals are clearly more equal than others. And just like the novel, we commoners are, as mere animals, inadequate to the task at hand without the lash of the state on our backs. That leadership requires special Animals that are superior to you and I. Yet knowledge alone leads to nuclear bombs; restraint, wisdom, and understanding allowed us to survive the Cold War without obliterating human life with them.

This is the chink in the armor of the Hard Left; they do not adequately understand the nature of understanding.

What is valuable may extend beyond mere facts or sheets of data. That is not the end all of how decisions are made. There is more to the story than just the recording of the observable, and those other forces play a vital force in life. They have meaning, and those meanings are the difference between life and death. The difference between living and not surviving.

The New Atheism cannot answer for all that is necessary for the creation of a successful society. It took thousands of years to get here, and everything in civilization is built up one block at a time. Family is by necessity at the center, as children begin the process to adulthood there, and spend more time away from public institutions such as the school as they spend in it.

From there, the child needs to be brought into a society that both provides rights and creates responsibilities owed back to the whole in return. That requires the society itself to have value and meaning to the new adult. Strong society is not just made of a mob of people attempting to survive. It is made of individuals who should be able to believe that the provision they receive is enough to require loyalty in return which they actually respond materially to.

Beyond that, people are mostly tribal; Iranians, Koreans, Japanese, Indians and many other nationalities have strong identities based on nationality. These are often so strong the people from these many places come to America yet retain their national identity first. Computers and smart phones and DNA kits have so far done nothing to undercut this tribalism, and there is no indication they will ever do so.

Soon, it is going to be necessary to rethink the ideas of the New Atheism and the American Hard Left. The tribalism that keeps those in America in their own communities has brought the specter of asymmetrical warfare to America and Europe through the Muslim community. The practitioners of Islam to a large extent have proven completely immune to the "seduction" of "modern life".

They see the Western lifestyle as corrupt and profane. They believe the only true religion is Islam, and look forward to a day when the whole earth is covered by a universal caliphate. Many truly believe this caliphate will arrive one day, one way or another. Jihadists see themselves as making war on the infidels that resist Islam, headed by the United States and Europe.

We then have entered a race to see if the power of technology can civilize and modify the Muslim impulse to domination or if the infiltration of the West will overtake the population of Europe, tipping the balance of power and largely isolating America and the ungodly population she holds. This great horse race will determine the future of our children's children. But we will know how the race is going in the next few decades or so.

It then becomes important to look closer at the ideals and understandings of the New Atheism and the Hard Left. Our future depends on what we do with the arguments and vision of those on the left. Time is short to determine if they are up to the task, and accept or reject their world view based on the reality of the situation we face. Europe is on the brink of being swallowed up whole as it's territory tips in the direction of Islamic control.

If the Hard Left and the New Atheists are correct, we must follow them completely. If they are wrong, we must shake them off wholly. We cannot get this wrong; a new Dark Age is nearly upon us if we do. We live far closer to twilight than dawn at this present time. Let's reason and wrestle with ourselves and determine a way to go, because if we do not, the way we are going will be determined for us. And that is a very, very bad thing.

CHAPTER TWO
A STAR WARS FUTURE

So which do you prefer, Star Wars or Star Trek? How connected are you to their stories? Are you evolved enough to appreciate the importance of those products? Answer carefully, your response may lead to death threats and suggestions to off yourself. This is serious stuff, and you can end up in real trouble with friends and family if you do not answer correctly. Strangers certainly will not take to you well once they know your insufferable opinion should you take the wrong view of this modern religion.

Serious stuff, eh? Life or death, quite literally. These are not just movies, or even entertainment franchises. To millions of people around the world, they are far, far more than that; they are the magic doorway to a very real, tangible, believable future. They are critical, the central canon to a world without a personal God, where mankind actually is the highest power in existence. You touch that rail at your own physical peril.

The modern Hard Left has developed a three-legged

ideology that becomes the lens through which they see the world. The first stool is postmodernism, the belief that all there is to human relationships is the struggle for power between different groups of people. The end of all human activity is power, and those who wish to have power must fight for it. This is a remnant of the old Communism, what was salvaged after the Soviet Empire began to show both it's age and it's cruelty.

When the Soviet Union fell, the left was still focused the struggle for power, but now without any real public purpose. So the public purpose became to give power to the powerless, though somehow in the intervening 40 years, this never seems to have happened. There are, however, two more legs of the Hard Left ideology, futurism and universalism. Futurism is well developed and publicly presented through science fiction, the message that science can and will eventually fix all the problems of mankind. And universalism, the acceptable form of pseudo religion provided through generic belief in life itself, as represented in Star Wars and similar less famous offerings.

This is not my idea. As Brian Young, who is a contributor to StarWars.com stated "Star Wars is religion. Even for those who have their own theologies, Star Wars reinforces it. For many people, these are serious and sacred texts that have helped them through as many problems in their life as the Quran or the Bible."(1) Star Wars is in every measurable way a modern religion, not much different than Christian Science, except without the Bible and without a meaningful God. It quite actually is a religion, and one that hundreds of millions of people all around the globe put their whole souls and belief into. They are true believers, just as much as any other religion.

That is the reason for the angry reaction to the latest

iteration of Star Wars - you are actually messing with people's religion. The new Star Trek movies have not suffered the same fate, because the current movies are acknowledged as an alternate universe rather than an extension of the original series, and Star Trek deals with a separate part of the New Atheist cinematic scripture than Star Wars does. Also the technical part of the belief was not corrupted.

Much as the Bible can be divided into separate sections, such as poetry and prophecy, Star Wars deals with the nature of the universe, and the nature of God. Star Trek is a lot like the instructional part of the Bible, informing the New Atheist movement about how to live, as an example of the perfect society based on New Atheist beliefs about the nature of man.

That is, the New Atheist movement does not actually mean a totally godless universe; they mean a universe controlled and empowered by a mindless, neutral "force"…THE force. There are many differences between the god of Star Wars and the God of the Bible. The claim that Jehovah is a creation of men is literally a fact to the religion of Star Wars.

The first big difference is that the god of Star Wars is impersonal. The force has no surname, it has no will, it is not worshipped, it is not appeased. It is not a he or she or anything at all. I guess that is one way to avoid gender pronouns, but it causes as many problems as it solves. Since it is an impersonal impetus to the universe, was it created at the big bang, or did it exist before? And if it existed before, how would it spark the big bang, not knowing what that would entail or how to do it? Power without direction is random like lightning strikes.

It is not knowable, not namable, not capable of

responding to the cry of the sentient beings it holds together. It is a river, constantly flowing from nowhere into nothingness. The modern version of the River Styx, if it flowed into the Great Lakes somewhere near Toledo Ohio. And it was on fire.

This impersonal force is not good, not in any real sense of the word. It has both a dark and a light side, much like Yin and Yang in Tao. But they are not the same; Yin is male and Yang is female, but the dark and light sides of the force are nothing…and really mean nothing if you think about it. They are of equal power apparently, which solves the "problem" of evil as it comes from the same source as good does.

So 6 million Jewish dead at the hands of Hitler? ….meaningless, just a part of the ever swirling loss and gain that takes place everywhere in the universe. Good does not win, but temporarily; the light side of the force merely flows to equal strength as the dark side. Somehow, they are supposed to "balance" one another to where life is not particularly good or bad. The ultimate office worker.

There is no higher power that is truly in charge, that allows evil to exist in a temporary state in order to both expose it's nature to all creation as a lesson to everything involved and as a contrast to the good of the Master truly in control. Instead, evil is not a problem at all, since it is not anything real. Life is just life, and death is just death. You and I dance across the river of time as meaningless cyphers, swallowed up in the river again upon croaking, only to reappear as a pineapple or perhaps a piece of melba toast.

Unlike the God of the Bible that needs to be recognized and approached, the goal of the force is control. There is no real faith, only focus. Reach out with your feelings, pick things up, aim your blaster, "see" with a blindfold on. Focus enough, and you can be like David Carradine, master of life, without all the groveling and humility and repentance and learning involved. Nothing here to chap the conscience at all. Become a master, and it is apparently possible to control the force enough to keep your consciousness after death. This is apparently a lot like the original Greek version of Hell….you exist in a vast void, with nothing to do except occasionally meddle among the living on the side you prefer. Imagine existing for all eternity in a cosmic waiting room. What a wonderful life.

But since the force is neutral, there is no real heaven or hell, just disembodied existence in nowhere. Of course, it appears only the "good" people who use the light side of the force get to live this wonderful disembodied existence. Somehow, the users of the dark side don't get the same opportunity, a giveaway of the real religious beliefs of the New Atheist.

For the New Atheism, this is the perfect answer to morality, as it is necessary to do nothing more than have faith in faith, that everything will magically turn out OK rather than believe in some imaginary man in the sky. Yet even here "good" according to liberal policy is rewarded, by being able to go floating through the eternal ether. But sin is not punished, as the evil simply dissolve back into the vast pool of meaninglessness from whence they came. The twisted, un-answering helmet that belonged to Darth Vader is the ultimate icon. It is the perfect religion for the small-believer, for those who want to believe in good without a personal source for it, a creator without a purpose, ergo no requirements. In this world it really does not matter if you help an old lady across the street or push her in front of a bus. It all only exists for the meaningless circular drama of life anyway.

Notice not everyone gets to experience the good; that is limited to those who have "evolved" enough to have the correct gut bacteria, at least according to the canon of Episode One. Midi-chlorians are given the excuse of being able to help the user focus the power of the force. The Holy Spirit is replaced…by germs. This is standard pabulum of the left, who believe in human social and mental "evolution". Being proficiently pro-whatever the left is promoting that week is a sign you are evolving, and have the correct mental probiotics in your system. As long as you do not think too hard and give yourself a fever which apparently will kill the little buggers. Who knew salvation just requires microscopic viruses without a brain? At least they resemble their hosts in that particular characteristic.

The rest of us, the un-evolved, get to live off the scraps churned up by the conflict between the dark and the light. We must be defeated, or at least kept in check. Is it any wonder then why the Hard Left see the state as a rightful surrogate parent? And since the state has a rightful claim of parentage, should it not then get to set the rules for it's children? Isn't this to a word what the Hard Left espouses?

This is subtle poison, and leads to millions adopting the idea of a neutral version of karma, where the good are rewarded not for the good but as a balance to the negative and the wicked are punished not for their wrongdoing but in order to even things out. In today's world an untold mass of believers spout this nonsense. We get to believe in our illusory control of our lives, while still getting to say empty-headed nonsense such as "everything happens for a reason" and "everything teaches you a lesson" - even though the lesson, and/or reason, are unknowable, being brought to us by an impersonal force that cannot communicate or contain meaning. Everyone gets off the hook, and should you continue your meth habit tomorrow, it happened for an imaginary reason that doesn't matter or to teach you an imaginary lesson that there is no reason to learn which is no big deal as long as someone else gets to live in a nice home in the suburbs to even it all out. Worse, the focus on emotions as the only valid filter for experiences cripples people.

Back in the late 1990's, I was privileged enough to get to attend Ohio Dominican College for one semester. And in my business class, we were taught by a Hispanic professor who had been incredibly successful - at one time running the factory that produced Kraft cheeses, like Velveeta according to him. On our first day of class, as part of this introduction, he took the bulk of the time to recount to us how he was once in the 1950's forced to sit in the back of the bus.

And it was quite a production; 40-plus years later he still choked up and wiped a tear from his eye. Never mind it had been literal decades since he had been through any such experience. Unless it was voluntary, it had been years and years and years since he had even been on a bus. He was a valued executive that had received excellent compensation from one of America's largest brands, and had undoubtedly been treated with respect by the company and it's employees. Certainly at the college no one was spray painting swastikas on his door.

But he was still, over 40 years later, an emotional cripple - no worse, an emotional slave, not just to the past but to the ideology that insisted he drink from his memory every day. I know it was poison, because he was blind, to both his present, in which things had changed almost completely, and to his future, in which such changes are practically guaranteed to be permanent and lasting. He was completely blind, blind to reality, blind to possibility, blind to hope. Blind to the human beings in front of him who were never his oppressors, just a room full of students. Hiding behind the government's skirt from a past that no longer exists.

What a hollow life this must be. There is no God to comfort the suffering or bring hope to the brokenhearted, just you and your inability to self-discipline your mind and regain the control that all the "more evolved" people who are clearly better than you have. Nothing but the struggle for power, so you can make sure no one can say mean things to you anymore (true or not). Star Wars is truly a part of the New Atheist religion, the central part of their new, narcissistic faith. But then, how should we live since we are no longer merely sinners but masters of the universe? That is where Star Trek takes over, describing the lives of Pope Kirk and Bishop Spock, as well as the tech healer, "Bones", along with the futuristic world we should all work to create. Over time the canon expanded to include their Star Trek descendants, ever more perfected and sterile.

On the Star Trek side, there is a metaphor for the Christian/Jewish God in the character of Q. This is not the God of the Bible, but the stereotype the New Atheists have of God. Q is really just a super powerful man, not universal but limited to one location at a time. While Q does have basically unlimited power wherever he is at the time, there are other like him, and he can be stripped of his power (and was at one point). Even worse, he has a whole load of bad character traits but none of the good ones. Q is boorish, self-centered, and obnoxious. He is no one to be worshipped, only suffered because the poor humans he harasses lack the power to shoo him away. It is the perfect description for the way the New Left thinks of the God of Abraham.

This image of tomorrow contains a critical mistake; the future is not about the people, but the technology. The people themselves are never anything more than confident, resourceful and proficient...servants. And completely bland. Insufferably, miserably, without any real passions or desires bland. Becoming almost nothing, they find themselves swallowed up in the literal belly of the technology they create. Here the individual becomes a ghost, a shadow with nothing more than a massive virtual reality game to interest them in off time, although there is also weird food that very little is made of.

And that is the problem with the Star Trek world. Throughout all the movies and series, at least when they are aboard the vehicles, there is a crushing blandness. You hardly ever see the food served to the crew. Whether on duty or off, everyone wears the same bland clothing, designed to differentiate rank more than anything else. The walls are unendingly grey everywhere they turn, even inside the individual bunk rooms provided to officers, apparently undecorated even though they are personally secured spaces from all indications.

That blandness continues through the personalities of the characters. Yes, in the original series particularly, Spock was needled by the others for his lack of passion and human intuition. But it is also clear that the others are more than a little jealous as well. And over time, the others become a lot more Vulcan acting like Spock than semi-human acting like Kirk. Yes, it is true they are more or less on military vehicles, but nothing changes when they are not. Spock's home planet is every bit as soulless as he is, and by the Voyager series, so is everyone else more or less.

In short, everyone becomes enwrapped in the

technology and stops being in any meaningful way human. Want proof? I have seen the bulk of the movies and TV shows (OK, ALL the movies) from the very beginning, and I do not ever recall seeing an Irish bar anywhere. Ever. Not even on Earth. And apparently there is no baseball or soccer either. No sports at all, except in a negative connotation. And children are never anything but problems, who when they are shown in the series or movies are mostly part of the crew and just as dull and bland as everyone else. While the life the writers create would be fascinating until we were up to speed on it, would you really want to live a life totally devoid of fun?

Fun is besides the point for those desiring a Star Trek future, the technology is the one and only goal. But unlike today, when games and entertainment are the bulk of the technology in use, the people of the future are more or less slaves to the technology and *it* uses them. It's more than making peace with it. Since no one needs to drive the trash trucks any more, since no one needs to be on the fishing boats, since no one needs to dig ditches or pour concrete, they seem to do little at all outside of the technology that runs their lives.

This blandness is intentional, and the writers make it clear they see a certain pecking order in the universe, with the emotionally barren human encyclopedias at the top of the food chain. Beneath the powerful and wise are the less evolved creatures, such as the Ferengi and the Klingons. Emotional and unstable, they are treated as the bad guys of the universe, because strong emotions are obviously nothing ever but destructive. From the very beginning of the series, this theme was explored in an episode in which a problem with the transporter split Kirk into two people, one basically totally violent and one totally pacifistic. In this original version of the story, it is intimated that the two Kirks need each other's attributes equally.

In Star Trek Voyager the same story is told again, only this time through the half Klingon and half Human B'Elanna Torres. But the story is different this time. While true the pacifist B'Elanna lacks the determination to survive on her own, it is clear the now fully Klingon half lacks the self control and focus of thought to succeed on her own. The story of the Klingons early on itself is basically one of what amount to Mongol hordes getting ahold of starships. They seem a lot more interesting in killing each other off by the time Next Generation was in full swing than anything else.

The real threat from the original series and much of the updated versions were the Romulans. Basically a little more than halfway along the scale between Klingon and Human, they have most of the self control necessary to be more organized and forward thinking than the Klingon ever are. In fact, they are a particular threat because they develop a cloaking device that can allow them to go mostly undetected. They use it the way bad guys always do, to cause trouble and try to run weapons which they did in an episode of Next Generation. Of course the evil bad guys are stopped by the unfeeling robot Data while he commanded a blockade ship for the Federation. What a coincidence.

Warf from Next Generation plays the part of the Noble Savage, the one who turns from his upbringing and natural impulses to become almost fully civilized. It's the most blatant version of cultural stereotyping I have ever seen, and that includes in real life. At one point Warf goes back to do his duty to his people during a civil war and by the end of the set of episodes is so disgusted with his fellow Klingons he practically begs to be allowed back on the Enterprise (I told you, I have watched LOTS of this crap).

But the worst are the Ferengi. There is no need to mention very many details of particular storylines, as they are nothing more that the sick cartoon characterization of what business people are. In fact, that's literally the background of the Ferengi. Their entire society is based on trade and business, and according to the writers of the TV shows, that society includes no redeeming qualities whatever.

Small in stature and shallow in understanding, they are the epitome of pettiness and unfriendliness. Everything is taken personally, and nothing breaks that small mindedness but their greed. They are misogynists, and often force their own women into prostitution like pimps would in Detroit. It is considered a high honor if you are able to sell your own mother. They have a sacred code called the Two Hundred and Eighty Five Rules of Acquisition that serves as the basis for their own society, a sick and twisted version of the Ten Commandments, as it is obviously impossible for a businessman to have any morals or values.

They disdain limits to economic power and worker's rights in order to exploit them. They are constantly scheming to gain an unfair profit from exchange. Even when they die, they sell their bodies to be bought as a remembrance to those associated with them. They even pray to a "Blessed Exchequer" and they bribe idols of him with money. In a lot of ways, they seem somewhat Catholic-like in their religiosity. They literally are the slimiest intelligent creatures imaginable to the left.

This is what the Star Trek future holds for those with ambition, slander and loathing. It is not made totally clear in the Star Trek world how the economy works, but it is abundantly clear it is nothing like capitalism. "Credits" are given to the crew and recognized as the human general form of exchange, but it is not clear if this means the government actually provides money to everyone or just to those directly employed by the government or a mixture of both. It is also not totally clear if personal ownership of business is allowed or widespread, because other than the Ferengi no information is provided. All the scientists seem to work for the government, which is surely the wet dream of millions of scientists and engineers and leftists across America.

The Ferengi federation is not considered nearly as powerful as the major powers elsewhere are. Roughly equal in technology to the Humans, the difference is indirectly attributed to the fact their system is capitalistic and the others are not. Even barbarians are considered better than businessmen.

Of course even the Ferengi can be redeemed, by adopting leftist human ideas, and in another example of cultural imperialism Ferengi culture is shown as "evolving" by adopting some leftist ideas as do the Borg. Interestingly, it is mentioned that the one ill the Ferengi never committed was allowing slavery or genocide. But the most disturbing part of this characterization is the indication the Ferengi are a stereotype based on Judaism. As much as the Star Trek future looks wonderful to some, it apparently still contains the worst of humans at this actual time. Remember, the New Atheist world is a hard left universe, in which everything is solved by technology.

In a fascinating divergence of ideas, the most feared protagonists early in Next Generation were the Borg, the physical blending of biological and mechanical systems into one unit. Ultimately, this is where technologists see the future of humanity anyway, so it is hard to understand the revulsion to the idea. In far too many ways to count it is this very uniformity and unwavering unity, at least on a macro scale, is exactly what the Hard Left looks forward to the most.

Considering the heavy investment made by those who follow the guiding light of the Star Trek Future in being serfs to technology and universalism of thought, the only area where it seems intuitive for such resistance would be in the ability to communicate. But even this seems strange, as the rights to communication are clearly of secondary importance to the Hard Left. There are some other arguments against assimilation as well.

One of those is that being assimilated is a lot like becoming a robotic zombie. This idea seems to strike a nerve. Of all the horror creatures to capture the current public imagination, nothing comes close to the modern zombie. They are at least in original form unthinking and unreachable in communication, because ultimately there is no person in the animated corpse of the person. Zombies are feared because they always kill, and because they can come from anywhere that people are buried.

But the Borg are not a lot like robotic zombies, because they are attempting to add to themselves through assimilating others. They are not mindless, but rather have a "hive mind" that seems to somewhat accept input as well as give orders. Others suggest they are scary because they are us, both literally and figuratively in many ways. They leave you no option, and everyone becomes a Socialist whether they wish to or not.

But the biggest part of the scare factor seems to be the idea that the Borg are a kind of a force of nature, much like the old Godzilla movies where science creates a counterforce by accident. The Borg are the natural outcome of the combination of biological and technological forces in sentient beings as they seek to add value and quality to their biological and technical life. The Borg is what happens when this process goes wrong, as it invariably will, and manages to wriggle free of the control of the biological species controlling it, just as Godzilla is in a more primitive form.

Now we come to the gist of the matter: Nothing scares the left as much as life after death. It is the most terrifying thing the Hard Left can imagine, for one overwhelming reason, the power of control. While people are living in their bodies, they can recognize some things such as floods and hurricanes as being beyond their control while maintaining the illogical belief that they are still in control of the bulk of their lives. Disease may limit this control, yet the person still remains, to whatever state possible. To an good degree they have a point; no one makes you live in a certain house or eat a certain food or dress a certain way in Western society overall.

Death cancels that false sense of control outright. Separated from the body, there is no way to prove the individual maintains control of their existence after death. Heaven and hell may very well be delivered by the judgment of a righteous God who cannot be challenged. In death, one goes from a world of comfort and self-centeredness to a world where the individual may feel they do not matter at all. It is all but certain that the bodiless life of the afterworld will be one that is inherited rather than controlled.

The zombie then, is the physical half of this liberal nightmare. It is the ability to live after death, with all that this implies, including the lack of control over one's world. To live after one dies is to be out of power, no longer the Lord and master making decisions or manipulating the environment as we wish. Like a newborn, the single remaining impulse of the zombie is to eat, to what end we never know. Do zombies ever crap, or do they just fill their bellies until they explode?

Once assimilation becomes a forced process similar to death, then on the biological level it becomes closer to an act of rape, stripping the assimilated of their ability to choose. And that is at least understandable, the revulsion humans feel to being violated. And to the Hard Left, nothing is more of a violation than to be forced to continue to exist after death. I think this is the best description of the Star Trek way humans see the technology of the future. But if this is the ultimate ends for mankind, then how is the worship of technological advancement the ultimate good?

How technology ends up being the answer to everything we are not clearly told, but this is a common and strongly held belief among the Hard Left. It is an incredibly childish belief, as nothing is ever made better or worse by the acquisition of technology. Technology is nothing until used, and we have used it to build society on one hand and kill 50 million people during World War II on the other. The assumption, based on nothing, is that as humans continue to "evolve" they will tend to lean increasingly towards using technology peacefully.

The ultimate assumption is that technology will spur further evolution in the human species, keeping us biologically superior to the technology created. The assumption is that by the time we reach the technological level of being able to become the Borg, the technology will still be far inferior to the creatures handling it. Also, it assumes that they will have the ability and resources to increase the level of innovation on a curve, leading us quickly to a level that will bring us non-believers to admit that the technology itself is the correct solution.

That is an awful lot of assumptions, and we have little evidence that most of them are likely to come true anytime soon. In the Star Trek future this is partially solved by being surrounded by multiple interstellar civilizations. Such a predicament would most likely force the nations of the world to unite, and the future background includes a world wide government, at least at the macro level, clearly with substantial if not universal powers.

This is the world your Hard Left neighbors are pining for, beginning here today, right now. And they have no intentions of compromise or kindness. They think technology is approaching a tipping point in our lives, and that getting to the Star Trek future from here is a lot more like rolling a small boulder downhill rather than rolling a large one uphill.

This blind, unthinking belief in the ultimate power of technology is the reason the Hard Left accepts their corrupt alliance with Muslims. They really believe that eventually exposure and absorption of the Muslims into leftist society is inevitable. It may take some time, but the process is not one that can be resisted. Keeping large populations attached to Western values is unnecessary, because even in the event of war, the aerial drones now in use are just the tip of the iceberg in the creation of an unmanned military force making human numbers unimportant.

How this will not spiral off into a dystopian dumpster fire we are not quite told. Who will keep the levers of control out of the hands of a military dictator, or corporate entities who could use it for their own gain? And what good does such a military do if the government controlling the automated force is dominated by Muslims who would gladly then use it to create the Caliphate they have always wanted?

From the Muslim view, they are in some ways like the Borg, and they see the conquest of Europe as just a matter of decades and numbers - and they may have a point. The bombing of he Ariana Grande concert has a much more sinister tenor when you realize the bomber had a strategy in the killing of young women. While in a pinch men are expendable, women are not, and every dead female becomes one that will never give birth in the future, tipping the scales a little bit more towards the Islamists. It is a form of playing the long game.

The hopes of the New Atheist are based on this single gamble; the inevitability of technology and the power it has to create behavior. They have gone all in on the idea. But even today that technology is quite often used effectively by those very enemies all around the world. And while we now continue to have a technological edge in the West, that gap has been narrowing. Beyond that narrowing, as nations adapt to technology they have managed to wrest control of the parts of the system inside their borders despite it's natural openness. This is most clearly seen in China and Iran, both of which have effectively gained control of their information networks despite claims to the contrary.

Even worse, it is not necessary to control technology to make use of it. Military weapons are bought and sold across the globe every day making control of the process of production less important. Likewise other technology be bought or shared even more easily, shortening the technological gap considerably for those who seem behind. We have seen this in North Korea and Russia, who despite somewhat limited resources have been completely effective in building new technology and hacking skills. North Korea has made incredible advances in nuclear and missile technology in a very short time, and both nations have been effective in developing groups of hackers capable of threatening the information systems of other nations.

It is not necessary to have a nuclear weapon if you can hack into the system of your enemy and control theirs. And while the game of electronic espionage has not yet reached that level directly, it may only be a matter of time. Imagine the movie Broken Arrow, only the enemy lives in a cave in Afghanistan, and we have no way of flushing them out. Instead of blackmail, the missile is launched, because the hacker is only after casualties. This is clearly a game the Hard Left has not thought fully through yet, and in the near future that may cost us all dearly.

The vision of the New Atheists and the Hard Left is to live a soulless existence allowing as much selfishness as possible while maintaining order and control through technology. They are the Brave New World of Huxley, and are unapologetic for it. Worse, they lack the intellect necessary to make it come about. For that reason alone they must be resisted with all our might.

1. Racism, Misogyny & Death Threats: How Star Wars Fans Turned to the Dark Side - By Brandon Katz • 05/16/18 6:00am   http://observer.com/2018/05/star-wars-fandom-toxic-disney-lucasfilm/

CHAPTER THREE
WHERE NOTHNG LEADS

My brief explanation of the three legs of the Hard Left philosophy is completely inadequate to explain the amalgamation of beliefs that make up leftist thought. Postmodernism, Futurism, and Unitarianism are only the bedrock layer of Leftist belief. From these bitter springs grows a vast network of specific beliefs the mangled likes of which Rube Goldberg could not have imagined in his wildest dreams.

From the simple to the absolute fantastical, Hard Left thought fills every space available. On the simple end are the Malthusians, many of whom have come to see the human race as nothing more than a bad disease making Mother Earth sick like a virus. Environmental alarmists, Black Panthers, feminists, La Raza, every sexual deviancy possible and thousands more specific beliefs sprout like the heads on the hydra.

Most members of the Hard Left are a bizarre mixture of these beliefs, and probably quite a few others I am unaware of as a decent everyday person. In fact, it is such a tangled web they are now dealing with "intersectionality" - they are finding conflicts of interest in the various "groups" they support, and need to develop some sort of hierarchy for the different interests. Is a pedophile higher or lower ranked than a MS-13 member from Guatemala? Does it matter if either or both of female? Who can tell?

Regardless of how the Hard Left decides to arrange it's imaginary world, the road to perdition leads to only one diagnosis, that of a sick society. Ideas can pollute a society every bit as much as a virus can pollute the body. Some of the wacky ideas that get bounced around in the general public are largely harmless; there is little damage done to society in belief in bigfoot or the Lock Ness monster or even UFO's.

Much more damage is done by rap videos encouraging white kids to commit suicide, and the craziness that surrounds the "resist" movement. Violence and oppression are meant to spread terror through the society in which they operate, and they also have more hidden and often nefarious side effects. We live in a world where social behavior is warped beyond any normal thought or right moral effort.

Take Japan, for example. On the one hand, they have issues that are not directly attached to anything faced in the West. They had their own culture long before the arrival of westerners, and the vast majority of their current culture is a modernization of classical Japanese ways to a major extent. Nobody makes the Japanese work 500 hours a week, they do that to themselves. But every type of "modernization" brings with it unexpected change, and Japan is no exception. On the surface Japan seems like a great place, as long as you have no intentions of working, dating, marriage, or raising children, or any other form of having a life. In a lot of ways Japan is our Star Trek future played out in real time.

Like every country washed along in the flood tide of leftist modernism, they find themselves reacting rather than taking control. And nothing signifies this like the marriage and childbearing rates in Japan. True, other nations, even in Asia, are facing the same issue. And theirs is not different. But oddly enough it is in the overbearingly private Japanese society that these issues are most openly apparent and played out in the public sphere.

It is important also to note that Japan was intentionally turned into the sick man of Asia…by Americans. It was the Americans after World War II that wrote the Japanese constitution. And the writers freely admit they intentionally made it as liberal as they could. In fact, the Japanese government was driven to be liberal 20 years before that same liberalism would fully burst out in the U.S.A. to the same levels. And they never had a voice in the matter as an occupied enemy.

Amazingly, the writers had no idea how their ideological theories would effect either nation, although now we do. And for both of us, we are close to the edge of not being able to sustain ourselves as nations, though it appears no one cares to do anything about it. I guess no one fights the dying of the light these days.

The pathologies are so deep and widespread it is difficult to know where to start much less make sense of it all. All the threads of society are so intertwined and tangled they make the Gordian Knot look like a weekend hobby. Not a single impulse - not a single one – seems come from a positive healthy place.

There are three toxic chemicals in the deadly brew of

modern relationships; feminism, sexuality, and social worth. Before we jump directly into this, I would like to provide you my understanding of what pornography and prostitution are today, taken from my book "David's House" for brevity;

"Beyond that it helps to understand the nature of pornography. I want to emphasize the fact that porn has always been fake; the actors on the screen are just that. They perform for the cameras, not for you. In the early days, porn was a teenage thing largely, mostly communicated through magazines like Playboy. But it wasn't given much respect or public space. The internet did not by itself change that. Instead, porn has gone from a barely tolerated evil to an acceptable part of society, but the reason for that acceptance shows just how fake and plastic porn really is.

Porn was always a deference to male sexual desire from the beginning. The difference is that in traditional society this deference is made reluctantly, because society has created solid means to have those needs met without porn. To a huge extent, this is no longer true, so the acceptance has to increase to meet demand if society is not going to uphold an honorable channel for those activities anymore.

But porn is still all a circus act. The woman in the video will never do that with you. And even worse, today's porn has devolved into nothing more than a cheap bribe. In today's Girl Power world, porn is just a toy to keep the men busy while the womyn set about doing all the important stuff. The modern "gaming" world is exactly the same thing. And the history of porn proves this beyond all doubt.

There was a time not so long ago when pretty much all women in America, both on the left and the right were unanimous in their condemnation of porn. They had the power to influence social standards, and they did. Do you know what year the Parental Advisory label was originally created? In 1985, with Tipper Gore leading the charge. By 1990, it was seriously starting to be used - two years later, over 200 albums had the warning label on the cover. Women were victorious in their crusade against pornographic materials in the public square, at least in music. It was well within their reach to force the makers of visual pornography back into the shadows as well. I have absolutely no doubt about this.

But that is not what happened. What happened was a huge change swept through women's culture in the early 1990's. And that change was reflected - not caused by - the very same Murphy Brown episode Dan Quayle so famously mangled the meaning of. Obviously the LA riots had nothing to do with Murphy Brown. But it was a peek inside how women were already beginning to change their views of men.

Before this, women were mostly focused on equal pay. When I graduated high school in 1982, the Equal Rights Amendment had been the focal point of the movement for a decade. Yes, the early radicals were there, but the bulk of thinking at the time was about economic power.

But that has clearly changed. No longer do women see themselves as equals but as superiors to men. And they have amassed incredible political power. They can destroy someone's future just by accusation in many social settings, and have penultimate power when it comes to marriage and divorce. Women made a choice about the time of Murphy Brown; they would rather consolidate their power over their children and child support and alimony than get rid of pornography.

Mentally at least, the vast majority of women have reduced men in their thinking to secondary importance. So video games and porn became pacifiers, a way to get men to retreat into imaginary worlds and not make noise in the real one. The divorced man needs to understand the girl on the screen isn't into you. She got paid cash. She is willing to be paid to smile and pretend so that your emotional scars can be soothed, and you can convince yourself that society sees you as a valuable member of your community, and that maybe one day you will find someone who will think enough of you to bed you again.

Just like blowing up fifty thousand Zorgath battle cruisers in an imaginary world allows you to feel powerful and believe you are intelligent and smart and a good strategist. You too can be a great general and heal your feelings of inadequacy and impotence at the low cost of some digital pixels, all you need is a gaming console. There is only one problem with all this nonsense - none of it is real. When you put down the video game, turn off the video, ask yourself this: "How did that make my life better? What did I accomplish?" I too have an X-Box 360. I play Rocksmith on it to become a better guitar and bass player. Not the same as a Zorgath battle cruiser.

I am not saying some escape is a bad thing. I use Facebook. I will go to the occasional movie and forget about the world for a couple of hours. I even pay some attention to sports. There is nothing wrong with that. But when these fake worlds begin to take over your real life, there is a problem. Because here is a truth; it is only the things you do in the real world that will make your life better. Maybe what you need is a second job. Maybe what you need is to spend time with your kids. Or your wife.

So what does this have to do with porn? That depends on what you think porn is. I think porn is a handout; it's a con job to convince lonely, unwanted men that better days are just around the corner, except they're not. That happiness (or at least sex) is not yet beyond their reach. Good luck with that.

So the man gets strung along, being convinced that women are not nearly as anti-male as they really are. And women, by offering the sacrifices of the sex industry to those men, get to maintain their innocence, or at least their space. Of course the girl in the video with those five guys isn't some man hating prude - she isn't going to be with you - but she obviously doesn't outright hate all men, and you have video evidence of that. It's kabuki theatre, on a worldwide scale. Those countries that block pornographic materials are wise.

It happens even more directly than that in Tokyo and Hong Kong and Nevada, the only drawback being it's just nearly as expensive as being married. The dirty little secret of our time is how many middle-class women worldwide are willing to look the other way and sacrifice little Thai girls as long as they don't have to deal with some nasty man every night.

And that's the truth.

The sex industry is fake. It exists solely to titillate and give you a sense of power. Don't believe me? Do a little research on how much rougher the latest porn is supposed to be compared to the early years in the 50's through 80's. Anything to pacify you and keep you feeling like a man. Even if it means helping you work out a little anger."

Did I miss anything?

This is certainly true, but even all of that is only the tip of the iceberg. What we are dealing with goes far beyond sex being used as a pacifier to keep men under control, although this is clearly demonstrated by the undeniable fact that both pornography and prostitution are much better organized, more publicly accessible, and much more widely accepted in general in westernized countries than in others. It is true this varies here and there, and there are some societies where other ways of providing sex are used, but those few exceptions do not disprove the very heavy weight of the rule.

Yet if you think about it, none of what I have been

describing is in any real way "sex". At best it is a crappy form of masturbation, and soon enough you won't even be sleeping with real women any more. Western-based civilizations have so allowed themselves to be programmed we have lost the ability to tell when sex is good and satisfying and worth the effort and when it is not. Worse, with the invention of robots even sex with limited fake interaction will be easy. This is at the very edge of the psychological universe, the place where as human beings we really are staring into the looking-glass, and ready to step into unreality. There are still other layers that extend beyond even this.

For example, let us turn our attention to the "Herbivore Men" in Japan. Once again, this is not a problem limited to Japan, as every western nation has a small percentage of MIGTOW men, who are shunning relationships and marriage. Further, this group of men are growing and vigorous. And there are some who fall under the "INCEL" acronym as those who are involuntarily celibate because they cannot find partners.

Society ignores these issues, and passes them off as personal problems. This is an empty oversimplification of truth that means nothing and fixes less. Yes, it is true that society has undergone massive changes in short order, and that some people have "adapted" to them better than others. But even this is just blather, really, because it is easy for someone who gains from social and legal changes to be happy about them, and that itself has nothing at all to do with "adapting". Scant few people "adapt" to negative and oppressive circumstances and go around pretending be happy as a bee afterwards, at least very few who are not mentally ill or completely brainwashed. And why should they?

The MIGTOW people are not even themselves totally

unified on what they are looking for through their resistance. There are some who monk, and swear off women totally. Other men swear off western women, but would be willing to try to have a relationship with a woman from a non-western source, in the hope that having not been brainwashed their entire lives will make having a relationship less overwhelmingly difficult. Still others are the pump-and-dump types, who spend their nights gambling the condom doesn't break. We call those men "parents".

But in Japan the whole table of sexual and relational dysfunction is spread out (pun intended) completely in public view yet it is even less healthy than in the West. And the range of options is nearly as wide as humanity could possibly produce. Japanese pornography ranges from the everyday to the outright disturbing, with the tentacled alien sex being both a well-known example and a totally mild version. It's truly mind bending to think of buying porn mags of this stuff on the street, and it is easy to think of Japan as being sex-crazy. Where else in the world can you attend a public penis festival?

Yet this outward show is as hollow as a bell. Beyond the TV, Japanese have less sex than anywhere else in the world. And it's not even close - 19% fewer of the people in Japan have sex than in the next least-screwing country, according to The Richest(1). And once again, we are only looking at the surface, there is even more to go over once you pop the hood.

Let's start with the list of the top ten countries having the least sex. There are some surprises here. Japan is not the only Pacific country listed, so is Thailand, New Zealand, Singapore and Australia. The rest are western countries, except one. Holland, Canada, the UK, and the United States are on the list. The only non-advanced country on the list is Nigeria.

So the vast majority of these countries have the same pathology. It is just easier to see in Japan, because the trend is so strong and the drama is played out a little more in public there. This issue is totally beyond just not getting married or having a regular significant other; we're talking about a majority of people not having any sex at all, of any kind. And men are far less interested than the women in any of it.

Could those men be lying to us? Maybe. In the west men have been expected to lose their virginity and be semi-public about it. The reverse could be happening in Japan, where there is pressure not to admit to having sex. But in America, surveys would reveal there was a difference between the men's claims and the amount of sex women claimed they were having, so that was easy to identify. In Japan it is not, and by all accounts the men are telling us the truth - they're just not into her. *Any* her.

How could the country that produces some of the most vile and perverted porn in the world not be having sex at all? I want to unpack this phenomenon from that starting point, as it will be easier to see how these problems radiate from one central issue starting here. And these effects spread out all across society, rippling through the entire population in one way or another.

I want to go back to the idea first proposed, that sex is disconnected from the natural flow of life in Japan, because that is going to be our theme, disconnection. What the individual Japanese person sees when they look at pornography, just like everywhere else in the world, is not seeing sex as normal people experience it, overall. And so that becomes the first layer of disconnect; sex looks like entertainment, not like the important part of a relationship or even what may happen at the end of a dinner-and-a-movie date.

That is why thousands of women can go to The Shinto Kanamara Matsuri festival and giggle and have their pictures taken while they suck on a penis-shaped lollipop and go home alone afterwards - because there is a literal disconnect in their minds. This unhitching, this separation of being human from our experiences and emotions as a human is a response to society accepting the idea that all human activity is artificial. It also reinforces the belief that the contribution of the individual is not important socially only personally.

Porn has the same effect in this manner on both men and women in the response of disconnect between pictures on a screen and real human interaction with real human beings as an activity. This disconnect spreads its way throughout society in a thousand different directions. It is part of the Anime scene, preferring cartoons over real people (we have similar issues in the west - much of this translates directly across societies).

From there it spills over into the cosplay scene, where the individual disconnects from themselves to become imaginary characters, just like at a Comicon festival in America. I would suggest it is hard for someone to think of themselves as fully real in the world while in this mental mode, and that it would be hard to date and become emotionally connected in a real way to someone with blue hair and wearing a cat woman suit whenever she can.

But this bubbles through society in a thousand different directions. Female pop groups (some of whom I like) often force the girls out when they are no older than 21 or so, and replace them with underage girls. There are literally teahouses and coffee shops where one can go to be waited on hand and foot by young ladies hired to basically pretend to be your maids. They'll even call you master.

And almost all of the bands and acts with women in them wear some sort of maid outfits on a regular basis. It goes on and on and on in many places of business and in many ways I know not about I am sure. The maid outfit has become the real-life Godzilla of Japan, overshadowing the entire city every weekend, crushing the future of the next generation, especially at the local music venue.

I have to admit to you it bothers me far more than you could ever imagine to have to criticize Japanese/Asian women for this. Compared to the tawdry and masculine looking western women, Asian women are like a tall glass of cold water in the middle of the desert. I absolutely love the fact that there are women *somewhere* in the world that still wear skirts when they are not on the cheerleading team or a live web cam. Women dressing in a feminine manner is pretty much a lost art around these parts.

The problem is real femininity isn't just about wearing skirts, or just about speaking softly and politely or just about not spitting tobacco. Real femininity, just like real masculinity, has to come from the very core of who you are, not just to yourself but who and what you are in the world. The desire to be feminine is to be a whole woman - with the attending desires for relationship and children included in part of what makes a healthy human whole as a woman, at least for the vast majority of females. This is not my belief, this is nearly universal among women everywhere else, and when asked, even Japanese women say they would like to get married someday. But that is an imaginary abstract someday, and they don't want to marry very badly. So they don't. Being a housewife polls highly as the desire of many Japanese women, but that is more like a daydream than a goal.

This is natural, and it is a self-evident truth proven simply through the fact that even in places where this disease of the feminine heart has taken root, the vast majority of women will still eventually have at least one child. They may not have more than that, but most will have one anyways. And even in Muslim societies where they are treated as little more than chattel, Muslim women are still willing to have families and children. We want to make word salads and endless psychobabble why what I am claiming is not true, but it's all a lie, uncovered by the reality of the vast majority of women in everyday life.

Don't think for a minute I am letting men off the hook here. We also allowed ourselves to be distracted with the shiny nonsense of modern society and ignored our own rights in our society because it is easier to keep our head down and be a good employee and quiet neighbor. Everyone seems to have forgotten they are more important than just some cog in a machine, and we have let women down, as we are unwilling to fight for ourselves much less fight for them. What did you expect them to think?

For the Herbivore Men, they are not just uninterested in women, they are just as ambivalent about Japanese work society. They see the long hours and the nonsense time spent drinking with the boss to not be worth the effort, and the lack of sleep, as well as the end result of turning over the paycheck to the wife at the end of the week as not being worth the sacrifice. And honestly, it isn't worth the cost. It just so happens this is no excuse for checking out and not fighting back.

This unhitching is something we can see everywhere we look. The Japanese are incredibly polite, but lack the weight of soul to believe in something strong enough to stand up for it very convincingly. Everyone swims in the same direction based only on being nice but there is no one thinking about the direction itself as a real thing and no one is in control of it. This comes not just from social pressures but from their history. The aggressive nature of the Japanese as a nation, from the opening of Japan by Commodore Perry to the end of World War II makes most Japanese shy about being aggressive.

So like many nations, they allow the pendulum to swing too far the other way, forcing themselves to be much too pacifistic and tame in order to avoid repeating the mistakes of their history. While this is understandable, it is no more healthy for the nation than the opposite was, and that pacifism is like putting sludge into the gearbox of an engine; it bogs the motor down from the increased inertia. A weak engine can't speed, but it can't climb a big hill either.

It is much like having a child that turns out to be a bully. On the one hand, you want your child to stop being so aggressive and adapt positive and friendly behavior. But becoming overly passive as a result is no more healthy than being overly aggressive was. It is necessary and healthy for a person to have the self-confidence to take up for themselves. Extreme passivity creates its own issues as we can clearly see.

This issue is also a matter of perception; for now, the Japanese do not see the effects of the decline in birth rates in ways that stand out. It is natural in advanced societies for the rural poor to desire to move to the city in order to increase their potential earnings, so in the cities there is not much of a change. What changes that have occurred have happened in the rural areas, where some small towns are practically abandoned.

Eventually those rural areas will no longer be able to provide enough people to the cities to keep up the population there, either. When rents in the big cities start to fall, they will do so because the population is no longer being reinforced enough to keep landlords from having to compete for tenants. Then, the end is relatively near. But as long as the cities are full, there is little motivation to act. Out of sight, out of mind.

Our first reason for the lack of reproduction in Japan is the disconnect between life and entertainment. Much like the ancient Romans we have become sated with our Bread and Circuses, and do not really see ourselves as keepers of the traditions and beliefs we were given through our heritages. A small but powerful number of people are Internationalists, who see themselves as no longer citizens of a nation at all but as citizens of the planet. Most of us do not go that far, but our attachment to our local citizenship has weakened in critical ways.

In the west, this habit is individual; most people "float", varying the amount of attachment they have to their local society based on what they desire to get from it. In Japan, it seems more like an internal disconnection on a national level. Japan is very much a homogenous society only for racial Japanese. But at the same time they seem to almost be observers to their own culture and not really emotionally involved participants. Being Japanese is just something they are, like height and weight and eye color. But it is something that they are only in looks and practice, but not in soul. They don't own being Japanese.

The next disconnect I wish to cover is the one created by feminism. I understand feminism is a taboo subject especially here in America, which stifles any realistic criticism or understanding of the effects of feminism on society. I am simply going to break that taboo, and you can hate it all you want if you must, but our societies are dying off due to the unrealistic demands of the Hard Left ideological movement and feminism leads the way.

The I wish to begin by covering the negative effect feminism has had on women, then we will move on to the combined effect all of this brings to the interactions between men and women. The biggest such effect is the disconnection of women and men from each other, the effect of which is much bigger on women than men, and works its way from the female to the male.

The first such effect I would like to discuss is the effect of female power in society. If you wish to read some material from men's rights sites, that will give you the rough idea of the issues men face. Here's the thing, though; most people don't spend the day worrying about 78% of all suicides being men. People respond to the reality of situations they face during the day in their own lives. If we apply this principle to the total activities of people in Western and Asian societies honestly, we will come to an astonishing conclusion, that women easily hold the bulk of power in the Western world and in much of modern Asian nations as well.

The Japanese habit of the husband turning over his paycheck to his wife ought to be a complete bellwether about how in general marriage works in Japan. There are some ways in Japan at least where women lack some power they should actually have. They should not be molested while traveling the subway. And I believe there is a way to be fair about rape crimes, but no nation handles that subject well right now. In America the opposite happens, and rape charges are often used as a personal and political tool of revenge. Real things matter more than any number of imaginary slights, but we do not call women out for rape charges made to get even for a bad relationship. And in America, we require no evidence at all when a woman claims physical abuse during a divorce, and men have no real rights at all in divorce proceedings.

Despite that, and the issues with riding the crowded subways with the men, how women see themselves is acted out in private and in public. The most important one of these is the amazing extent to which Japanese women and men are perfectly happy to not have any interactions with each other at all. Some will laugh at the idea that women wandering round with only female friends on a Saturday night is any type of problem.

Don't laugh too hard. Let me make a couple of observations to clarify. First, that all those women are comfortable doing that is a signal that in Japanese society, despite the uniformity, women have become atomized in society. It's not the same kind of individuality as in the West, but as far as the right to participate in general public activity outside the workforce it is not questioned. Unlike in the past, parents do not interfere in the romantic relationships of their children nor seriously pressure daughters to marry. And neither does society.

The result is the same as it is for the attachment to nation; women seem to "float" semi-detached to the desire for relationship and family. They say they want these things, but every weekend settle for spending time with girlfriends. The same thing happens in the west, but in America, marriage and children were such a central part of culture for so long that even today a large majority of women still expect to be married, and they engage in activities such as dating on a more serious level. But even here, marriage rates and expectations are in steep decline.

Adults in first-world countries will point to the cost of

childrearing as the reason they do not marry/do not have children. I don't believe it for a second in the terms provided in the excuse. Claiming children are expensive actually means something completely different. It is really a person making an open commitment to selfishness. The cost of having children is calculated by the greedy not the committed.

I know this is true, as all around the world, hundreds of millions of poor people have children every day, and manage to raise them as best they can. Poverty is an uneven concept and for much of the world poverty means living in a small village as a farmer. It may be a rough life, and people in those circumstances may not get much monetary recompense, but as poor farmers most children these days are not totally deprived. Disease is a much larger threat to children in nations that do not have strong communications and health systems than hunger.

First-world people who use the excuse of cost really mean children require a lot of sacrifice. And this constitutes a real problem for those who do not want to give up all-night online gaming sessions or Sunday brunch with the girls. Single people spend their money on themselves, their time doing what they want, and it is the immaturity of the person that does not want to make the permanent, life-limiting sacrifices necessary to have a family that is really the problem here.

That any children at all are born in first-world nations only goes to show how much marriage and children are a part of the female psyche in it's natural state. But even here in the West, the trend is for women to have the children but not the husband. This is particularly true in the black community in America, where the actual family is in collapse. So we are in a weird netherworld in which women to a very large extent live their entire lives atomistically even in childbearing.

So women now have come to a point where they no longer see men in the same way they used to. Men are no longer looked at as life partners to anywhere near the level they used to be. And even women who do have children in the West have unchecked power over the rights to the children, so they have no reason to seek the same kind of attachment to men their mothers and grandmothers did.

Men then become this secondary tribe they live among but not with, with no real motivation to close the gap. And since the average woman is not thinking of long-term planning with a man, they feel much more secure holding out for the cream of the crop.

This limits the number of women available to the average man as only 25% of the general population of women is available to the everyday male. One quarter are not interested at all in family, one quarter are among the few that still do attach - and obviously already have a man, taking them fairly out of play, and the last quarter go the child only route.

This is reinforced by the way women talk about themselves in public and in private. They use terms like "queen" to describe themselves. They openly claim their superiority to men, and make clear they have expectations to be served. Even the biggest, fattest, pimpliest, toothless woman in America thinks her amazing, incredible self deserves Brad Pitt, and will actually hold out for nothing less. They don't have the time or patience for us mere humans. Just listen to how these women talk about themselves on social media.

So only about 40% of men have any real chances of creating stable relationships with women, and that is fraught with danger, because women do not come with tags like a mattress telling you the woman you are with intends full commitment or has the character and emotional availability to pull it off. It is the ultimate kind of Russian roulette, and it usually costs the man his life eventually, just like the pistol version.

On the men's side, confusion reigns; they are charged with wrongs the vast majority of them never commit. They are welcome, but only a little, and for short periods of time. They receive indifference and anger in return for their engagement. And after a while, they respond by being no longer willing to engage. On this I do not blame the men at all. As I have mentioned, women have gained much power, and men have been left pretty much bereft of any real value. It is more likely the average woman sees the average man as more of an issue than an ally.

The effect of both pulling away on one hand and pushing men away at the same time has created a huge chasm between the two parties. Men have no ability to cross it, and women have no motivation to do so. Guess where that leads us? Right back to the sex part. The lack of sex in Japan is an issue of lack of interactions overall between men and women. Without flashing cash no women has ever been picked up by a man she didn't speak to. Think about it; you can buy porn on nearly every street corner in Tokyo, yet they have a T.V. show where men and women are brought together to kiss a member of the opposite sex for the first time. At the end of the show, there is a place where the man and woman are to go to if they would be interested in spending more time together. The men invariably show up, but the women almost never do. They got their 15 minutes of fame, and reinforcement is all you're looking for when you're a queen.

And so here we are, and there is no way to make it

better, except to pressure women in some way to fix it, to try to change social thinking on the subject of total female independence as a negative thing. But that will never happen, as I will safely bet the farm that women will not put up with that for a minute. It is just human nature that social groups who gain power will not relinquish it without a serious and bitter fight.

But there is also a moral reason; we have put women on such a pedestal that they actually are convinced they are completely superior to men. Through our own actions, we have fully persuaded women of their superiority, every bit as fanatically as a faith preacher in a tent somewhere. And that is the lid on our little morality play; we were wrong, but lack the power to change course, because society did the equivalent of pulling the cord on an inflatable boat with an air pack while diving in the middle of the ocean, and now it is headed for the surface whether we like it or not.

Women are in no way at all better than men. Women willing to work multiple 10-hour (or more) days in a row making porn for a paycheck will not spare 3 hours a week doing the exact same thing – *the exact same thing* – for their husbands. Why? Because it's free. I am trying desperately hard in these books to explain and encourage and not just name call, but for the life of me the only way I can describe this situation is defective. There is something defective about the way people in modern society choose to abuse their sexuality. There is something defective in the way men have responded by becoming an army of introverts bringing flowers to their favorite porn stars as a sign of a fantasy life out of control – and a real life that doesn't exist.

There is a meme floating around the internet that shows the living room of a man who is single. There is nothing in the room but a recliner, TV, and gaming console. Women bash the picture asking, "Is this OK?" as a backhanded insult. Other than my thoughts on gaming, of course it is OK. Single guys don't need much. As long as the owner of that living room has some beer and hotdogs in the fridge, he can have a pretty good summer.

All that other stuff, the nice houses in the nice neighborhoods, the nice cars (maybe not so much the car itself), the nice clothes and art and all that other stuff – we only do that stuff for you, ladies. We don't care nearly as much about it as you do. I would rather be hiking.

Almost all of civilization was built for your comfort, ladies. Men have created every modern convenience to see to it you are as happy and comfortable as possible. I am not saying it is only for you of course, I use the bathroom occasionally myself, and I appreciate indoor plumbing. I am certainly not gong to give up toilet paper anytime soon. And if all that was not enough, you asked for a paycheck, so we have worked hard to ensure that you have been able to join the workforce as well.

Unfortunately, the response to providing a nice soft nest for you is to your adding barbs and thorns and miles of razor wire to it. There is no positive response from women, only the ultimate twisting of the most basic instincts of human relations to some tawdry sex industry that promises the world but like everything else the left touches delivers nothing real at all.

It is not unreasonable that when your husband gives you a nice diamond necklace for Christmas that you are nice to him for the *entire day*. Despite the stupidity you have been taught gratitude and cooperation are not signs of feminine weakness. There is nothing wrong with expecting you to partake in some of the activities we enjoy, and I doubt it is especially difficult for you to sit on your ass in the ballpark and watch a Diamondbacks game with your man.

And I can absolutely vouch for the fact that there is nothing wrong with learning to love your family and husband instead of just raising the next generation of girls to be men, and 11-year-old boys to be playthings for your homosexual allies.

https://www.breitbart.com/entertainment/2018/12/19/11-year-old-dances-gay-bar/

And a little boring, everyday sex with your husband is not out of line either. If you are bored, that's your fault. Why don't you try to learn how to get a little fun out of life, even sex, instead of using your time trying to program everyone around you. No, this is all defective, from beginning to end.

The result of this dysfunction will eventually be the end of the first-world nations. Probably within the next twenty years, the first European country that was previously majority-European will fall to become a Muslim-majority state, with the rest to slowly follow over time. Here in America, the supplanting of western peoples with Latinos will continue, while in Asia the advanced countries will become a mere shell of themselves without some sort of massive immigration.

We are headed the way of the Spartans, who ended up being nothing but an amusement park attraction by the time the Romans arrived. Even the circus tent signs were worn and battered by then. You can call me all the names you wish, racist, bigot, whatever. It doesn't matter, the numbers are true and every person a liar. It's not just Japan, but South Korea and China and Taiwan and other nations in Asia that will hollow out in population over time.

It's amazing to me that we have not taken a hard look at what we have done. I would suggest even a massive amount of panic is in order - and there are places in Europe that agree with me. But we are so overwhelmed with distraction it all seems like a meaningless game for far too many of us. Our pain is soothed by our little screens bringing us unlimited access to nothing real. The terrorist attacks on the West are meant to hurry this process one tiny chip of population at a time. The only problem is, it's not necessary to have a helping hand. We are committing social suicide quite well on our own, thank you.

The beliefs of the Hard Left have offered us nothing, in exchange for a beautiful dream somewhere in the future where everyone is seen as equal, though no Western people may live there. Nothing wrong with equality in itself - but it has to mean something in particular and be worked out in sustainable and maintainable ways. And it has to be adjustable to reality rather than rely on the calcified principles those on the Hard Left are committed to. We have been given vacuity in exchange for our children's future, and it leads to our extinction, sooner rather than later.

Congratulations.

However, gentlemen, if you think I am going to let you off the hook here, you are out of your minds and don't know me at all. All of this - every single bit of it - is your fault, and yours alone. Even today. You have individually and collectively turned your back on the nation and civilization that has given you everything, and that is completely inexcusable. And being a fellow man, I know exactly what I am talking about. I lived through all the changes, starting high school in 1978. I remember it well.

We call them the greatest generation, but your failure was built on their backs. Americans coming home at the end of the war made the horrible mistake of believing it was over - they had won, and that was the end of that. There was little left to do, but go home and relax again. The Cold War was worse for the threat of nuclear annihilation than it was for any real threat of a ground war. The crude Soviet aircraft and ground weapons were never an even match with American equipment or tactics, a gap that grew after the Viet Nam War, to which we only ever partially committed.

Men let their guards down, and turned to the subject that the supposed victorious often do; themselves. During the 1950's and 60's men decided they preferred entertainment to family, cocktail parties and the cheap women that come with them or through Playboy to responsibility. With no world to conquer, men pursued their own interests, abandoning their children and families and society for drugs and alcohol. Not everyone, but a plurality, enough to fracture men's place in society.

Only by the 1980's there were no more cocktail parties with ugly turtleneck sweaters, only shabby alcoholics and half-dead drug users shooting up neighborhoods and living in shelters or under bushes. Yet instead of remembering they did this to themselves, men choose to blame others; the drugs came from the CIA, not the drug lords they made fabulously wealthy. It was not their fault they could not hold a job or pay a bill, it was the government not providing enough free cheese.

Through it all, little by little, men not only gave up on their responsibilities but on their rights as well. It mattered not they did not see the children they brought into the world but cared so little about. They did not care about society, seeing themselves as victims and not the problem. Men grew even more callous and unrealistic in how they understood their place in the world. Eventually we have become the very caricature of which we have been smeared; single men in greasy apartments with nothing but a recliner and a TV connected to a gaming console in the living room, with no real interests or plans for the future.

Men in relationships turned their backs on their fellow men, ignoring the pain and destruction caused by modern divorce laws, only concerned about getting their own as long as they could until it happened to them. It was only the lucky who avoided the ruin of divorce over the last few decades. Yet at every step, men went along willingly and gave up their civil rights without a peep. Not once have we ever claimed that our feelings are important. Men were so wrapped up in the imaginary "freedom" they were "experiencing" they never once considered they were losing their real-world freedom.

Every bit of this nonsense could be fixed should we ever decide to be men again. We're not depressed - we're just bored. How can someone be depressed about a world they really don't live in? Most men these days are far more attached to the fake digital worlds they spend most of their time in rather than the real one they complain about too much. It's a lot easier to fix things in a digital world with a few button presses than it is to fight for yourself in the real world. However, just like at every step that came before it, it leaves men and only men responsible for checking out….we've been doing it for 70 years now.

If you really cared, every MGTOW proponent would meet one Saturday a month, every month, at the state or local court house to protest and fight for our rights. If we really wanted our rights back, we would stand up for ourselves in the conversation of the public square, even if it means getting up in people's faces. If we ever want to be men again, we simply have to take off the dresses and take back our masculinity from those we gave them to.

Should we choose not to do so, we ourselves will be pushed aside as we always have been, as the powers that be are not going to make an army of soy boys either. They are going to make that army out of men who show a fighting spirit. Should you continue to hide behind your digital blankie, you will be continue to be pushed around for the rest of your life, with no hope for the future.

The feminist dream of a fully gynocentric future will not be fulfilled. Eventually the West will fall to the Islamic surge or create a way to defeat the Muslims. Either way, things are going to change, and the time is drawing nigh. Women and men are fully in charge of themselves in the West, and now must make some hard choices about the future. I would like to suggest you choose carefully.

Very, very, very carefully.

(1)
https://www.therichest.com/rich-list/poorest-list/the-10-least-sexually-active-countries/

CHAPTER FOUR
THE TRUTH ABOUT TWILIGHT

Humans are easily fooled. Some of us are skeptics, giving a frowning face to all the beauty cream commercials that claim they can get rid of all our file lines and wrinkles. The rest of us, we are just plain suckers for that kind of stuff. I am bald, so I understand men calling the 1-800 number for the magic new formula that promises to make your hair "seem thicker and fuller overnight!"

But while humans have made a lot of progress over the centuries, the vast majority of it has come in the last couple of hundred years. We went in less than 200 years from sailing vessels and muskets to spaceships and landing men on the moon. I am afraid we have exchanged the idea of knowledge for real understanding.

Truth is, we have not had all this stuff long enough to actually measure the vast majority of consequences our new toys have on the life and quality of our societies. We are literally still living in twilight, and it will be a long time into the morning before most things become apparent.

"Experts" do not see it this way and it is difficult to find one who has the self-realization to pause and not be so sure of themselves.

This at times leads to a hilarious merry-go-round of nonsense; eggs are bad for you, then they're not. A bowl of oats is good for you, then it isn't. We were headed for another ice age not so long ago, now the whole planet is about to burst into flame. One can start to wonder if the college-educated know anything at all.

Let's focus in on a particular example of this folly; the claim by Steven Levitt that abortion lowered the crime rate in America, a claim that made him famous through his best-selling book, *Freakonomics*. This is at best a non-starter of a theory. Here is the truth about Mr. Levitt's claim; there is no correlation between abortion rates and crime. Not only is there no correlation, there is clear and longstanding proof now that the claim is not true at all.

It only takes a little research to blow up this empty proposition. First of all, crime rates did different things in different states when abortion was legalized. The statistics for crime and abortion are both skewed by the left-leaning major metropolises on the east and west coasts. What happened in the middle looked nothing like that at all.

In Kentucky, the crime rates hardly budged in the high-crime period of the middle sixties to the early nineties. In Colorado, the crime rate bumped up, but did not have a sustained rise in crime(1). Hawaii, on the other hand, saw an explosion of the crime rate *at the time* abortion became legal, and did not come back down to 1950's levels long after the crime rate and abortion rate in the rest of the country had fallen considerably. In fact, it is still higher than it was in the decade before abortion became legal. See the graph on the following page.

So what are we to believe about this situation? That the state of Kentucky is full of the Holy Spirit who drove thousands women who were going to have demon seed to abort their babies? Or maybe the whole state of Hawaii is ruled by the Devil himself from a throne in one of the volcanoes and he possessed thousands of women to give birth to bank robbers and drug dealers slinging crack from the back of mommy's station wagon?

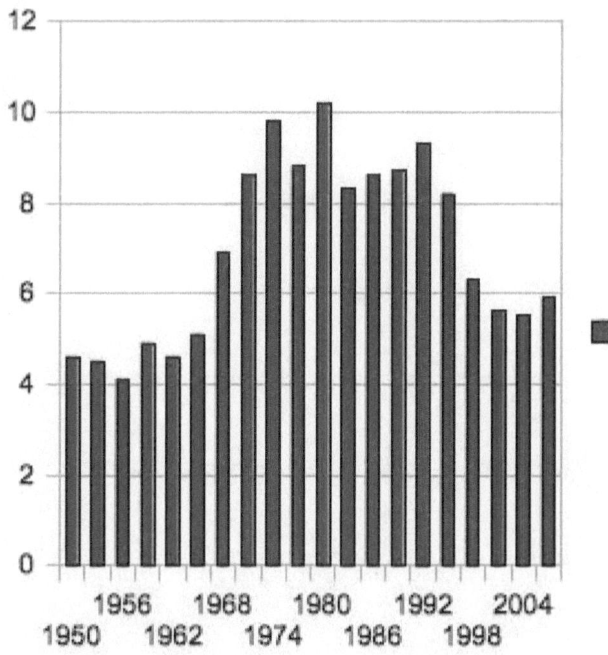

Crime Rates in Hawaii, 1950-2007
Source: Crime in the United States, 2008, FBI, Uniform Crime Reports

What kind of silliness is this? It is completely unreasonable to believe that all the women of the entire state of Kentucky all aborted the bad babies while in Hawaii all they aborted were the good babies. If you believe that, I have a bridge in Brooklyn to sell you, and you don't even need to have cash; I'll let you pay by credit card.

Here is the worst part; by 2005, when *Freakonomics* was published the crime and abortion rates had both been falling - simultaneously – for long enough that Mr. Levitt almost certainly knew that his claims were not likely to hold water…but he published his book anyway. Because you can do that in the twilight, when the answers are not so clear.

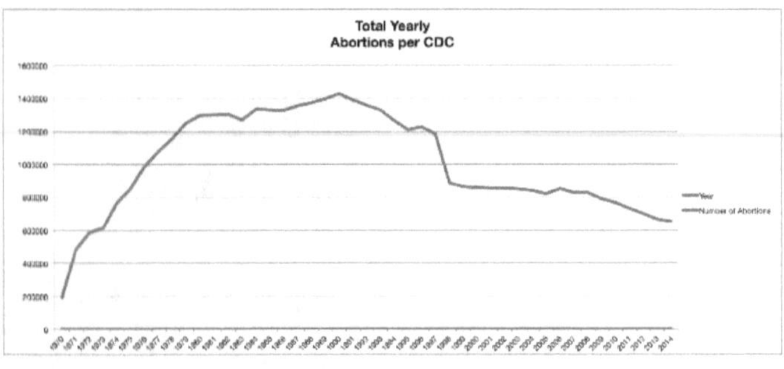

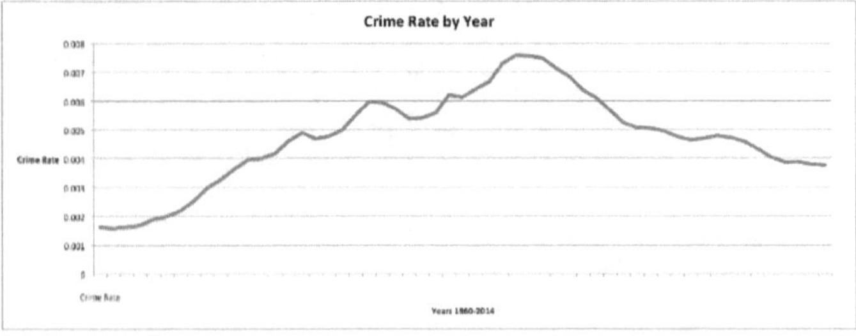

But far be it from me to burst your bubble; I'll let the Federal Government do that. Interestingly enough, the number of abortions peaked in 1990 (though the abortion rate had started falling in 1980 or 1981) and the crime rate peaked in 1991. Since the peak, both the crime rate and actual number of abortions have fallen together every year, abortion by about 40-45% as of 2014 and the crime rate by about 35% or so over the same time period.

At this point, it has been 28 years since the number of abortions have peaked(2), and 27 years since the crime rate has peaked(3), long enough now to say without a doubt abortion rates have absolutely no effect on crime. If higher numbers of abortions would lower the rate, then lower numbers of abortions should cause more criminals to not be aborted, and at some point the crime rate would rise again, and this has simply not happened.

These numbers are directly from the federal government, with abortion stats coming from the CDC and the crime rate from the FBI. I did nothing but get the raw figures and graph them, with one exception; California stopped reporting abortion rates in the late 1990's, so I added 25.7% back to the number of abortions at the end. Those numbers can be found in the third graph. And as you can see the abortion rate still continued down.

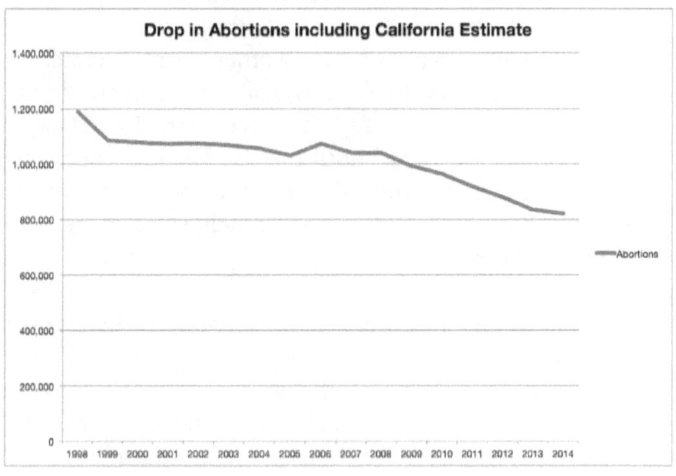

Obviously Mr. Levitt could not predict the future, but that is the problem of our twilight world; even the most sincere and honest "experts" regularly and consistently blow it. According to the Smithsonian magazine, fewer than half of 100 psychology studies could be replicated(4). So why do experts in this stuff talk with such confidence?

That is the great problem with living in twilight - no one can see clearly so people pretend instead. And it allows ideologues to fan the flames of emotion in the general public based on some pretty shady beliefs. But those beliefs are treated as fact, and taught as if they came from the very hand of God, not as if they come from fallible people who don't really know.

Next century, should our offspring beat back the challenge of Islam, we will be the laughingstock of the entire world. They will see our paranoias and emotional outbursts and wild swings in public belief and discourse as the irrational babbling of children. And in that assessment they will prove hilariously and factually correct. We are yet children, and have almost no idea who we are.

We have despite our advancement barely scratched the surface of any kind of knowledge at all, even about our own minds. Take the LGBT movement. Lady Gaga may sing "Born That Way" until the day she dies, but that will not prove it to be true. Proof comes not from songs, but from scientific understanding, which is nowhere near as perfectly clear(5).

The problem is we live in a society where those in academia and media truly are ideologues who have a preconceived version of the world and intend to sculpt public thought to their beliefs. They are far more religious than the average believer could ever be and miles more the actual child of hell than the worst Scientologist. But here in the twilight, it can be hard to see the text clearly, so they can get by with it. No one knows what the future will bring, but it is becoming clear that the bulk of it will not turn out the way the Hard Left and New Atheists predict.

But here we are in New Athens, almost exactly like the ancient Athens of the Histories, we are little more than a mob gladly putting our entire future into the hands of those adequately eloquent, as if big words mean they know something common sense and common observation does not teach people in general. Let me clue you in; they don't. Unfortunately it is our fate that just as we need voices of moderation, none can be found.

We are just like the Athenians or the pompous Europeans of the brink of World War I or the children following the pied piper. If we like the sound of the siren song, we will gladly follow it to our destruction. We have replaced reason and logic with our wants and emotions, which cannot turn out well for us. But as long as we are happy and entertained, we are determined not to allow ruin to distract us.

Just like the ancient Athenians, we are only like this due to our prosperity and sense of security. We also believe we have high walls for a defense from our enemies. Thus it comes as a shock to the Germans and the French when Muslim mobs burn cities but not to the Hungarians and others in eastern Europe. Familiarity breeds knowledge.

We should see the warning signs, but will not. We get angry when the ambulance siren drowns out the song of easy peace and cheap prosperity. We blame the victim and electronically murder our prophets. The corrupt kings of ancient Israel would be proud.

So off we march like little ducks in a row, to a future we know not what. Our rose colored glasses blot out the stars of twilight. History teaches us that nothing will destroy more surely than denying the truth, so we gave up history long ago.

But this is a turning point in the world; the sun may rise on humanity or it may set, depending on the direction we go. We do not see clearly in the twilight, and may be going in the wrong direction. It is a shame we are too proud to admit it.

1.   http://dcj.state.co.us/ors/stats3.htm

2. https://www.cdc.gov/mmwr/volumes/66/ss/ss6624a1.htm?s_cid=ss6624a1_w

3. https://ucr.fbi.gov/

4. https://www.smithsonianmag.com/science-nature/scientists-replicated-100-psychology-studies-and-fewer-half-got-same-results-180956426/

5. https://www.theatlantic.com/science/archive/2018/05/twin-epigenetics/560189/

6. https://www.usatoday.com/story/news/2017/06/16/born-way-many-lgbt-community-its-way-more-complex/395035001/
amazinghealth.com/13.06.24-identical-twin-studies-prove-homosexuality-is-not-genetic

CHAPTER FIVE
THE GOD OF SOMETIMES

The atheists have a point; far too often, God remains hidden, unknowable, unreliable. One person is prayed over and leaves the hospital the next day, as another is prayed over and sent to the morgue the next day. God seems spurious and fickle and distant even on a His best day. On a bad day He seems absent, like a parent that ran away from home and left the kids at the house all alone.

Answers are few and far between. Being trapped in time, we can't actually look forward and see what is best, even for ourselves. All we can do is see our current needs, and what we need in a generic manner to prosper in the future. We are vague, and so is tomorrow. I am reminded of a story I was told about certain parents who were told that their baby girl would die, never seeing her first birthday.

They immediately toiled in prayer to God to spare their daughter. Word was sent out to the denomination they belonged to for prayers from others. They all prayed mightily, and eventually received the good news their daughter would survive. But that is not the end of the story, because happy endings don't happen in this life so simply.

When their daughter grew up, she became a drug addict and prostitute. Her parents were no longer able to reach her, and all their prayers were now unheeded. What seemed a blessing turned to a curse, as often happens in the world. The good in the moment was outweighed by the pain and misery accumulated over time. God's mercy has a cost of exposing you to other obstacles over time, and then where are you?

Assuming God's goodness is so hard because it is so opaque, hidden almost altogether from our view. But that is the least of our objections. We look at the world and ask a perfectly reasonable question; so why doesn't God involve Himself more in the general activity of our days? Why not provide a shove, help us get a little further down the road? Why allow so much suffering?

I and millions of other believers would say He does, and there is a four way process through which this happens. The occasional miracle is only one of them. There are also three more; principle, conscience and motivation. It is apparent in human psychological makeup that we in general follow this, and we can acknowledge it.

The Bible says that if you don't work you don't eat. And this is a rule we almost all follow; even atheists have jobs. For people who are unemployed through no fault of their own, we provide some support. But we live the principle here as active agents in the world - being God's hands in it, believer or not. And there are lot of principles like that; don't murder, don't steal, don't sleep with the bosses' wife.

Then we all have conscience (used or not). The command not to murder is acted on by society through courts and lawyers and prisons, because the vast majority of us internally agree with it. It's our value because it's *our* value. So we may not all keep the Sabbath, but there are others we do have in the conscience. It is our fourth leg to the table that is really the weakest, for our emotions are meant to provide us motivation to hold to the other three.

The problem is the emotions are easily manipulated. A slick talker can turn a nations' anger towards the Jews or Christians or blacks or any of a thousand groups. Worse, we humans are not very good at discerning when we are emoting our beliefs from fear or proposing out of reason and logic or compassion.

Under the Hubris chapter I review the Histories by Thucidides but I wish to mention it here, because just as in Nazi Germany and Soviet Russia, an emotional impulse shared by a crowd can cause them to work just as energetically towards a negative end as much as towards a positive goal. Public excitement is often used to direct public activity as it did for the Athenians deciding to invade Sicily even if in error.

There is a statement you will hear me use over and over; you emotions are meant to be a tool, not a compass. A healthy person is not someone who allows their emotions to direct them, but who channels their emotional life through their intellectual structure of the world and their personal values. Cold and unemotional is just as dysfunctional as the emotionally unstable. Worse, they still have an crippling effect in the heart, whether blanketed off or just suppressed, just as we saw in the chapter on sex and relationships.

Today is September 3, 2018 when I am writing this particular section of the book. I have been unemployed since March 23 when I was laid off from the University of Phoenix. I have applied for over 1,100 jobs at this point in my job search. I have written one book, fixed another for print, and released a demo of my first song. It has been amazing.

Yet I am also running low on money. I haven't become rich and famous from my work. Six weeks from now I could be homeless. I can see God's timing and support in what has happened so far. But I can also see that hardship is possible just around the corner. Yet here I am typing away on my computer like nothing is wrong. Surely I am crazy.

The New Atheist would ask me a perfectly reasonable and intelligent question; "So where is your God then?" And I have to tell you the truth - I don't know. I don't know where God as at in the current part of my situation. I don't know what will happen any more than anyone else. I don't know why I did not find a new job four or five months ago. I literally don't have an answer, and neither does anyone else. Any Christian that says they do is lying and is not speaking for God in any way.

So the Atheist is right to have some scoffing at my trust and relaxation. But here is the thing; I have every reason to believe I am going to end up with a new job tomorrow (I actually started a new job on September 11th). There is more than me just deleting my funds and applying for jobs. I have also had interviews. and there are two jobs I could be offered first thing in the morning. We'll see.

The Atheist then is completely reasonable to ask me why I believe in God at all. What I am talking about is sounds completely random. Spin the wheel. Where it stops in no way is determined by a guiding hand. My results are no better than any others.

This is true in some ways, and for quite a few reasons my results have actually been below average, being older. I am nowhere near as far along as I should be financially and career wise. The more effort I put in and the more I produce the larger the deficit grows. I will likely never have enough to retire comfortably. Frankly it doesn't look very good for me.

I do however have two good answers to their objections. The first one is I have seen God move before. Specifically move before. Literally make something out of nothing. At Christmas time. Let me tell you the story of How God Saved Christmas.

When I was married in the early 1990's, we lived in pretty cheap housing. Our rent was only $250 per month. We were actually doing pretty well at the time, comparatively speaking, and both of us were working. My ex-wife's mother lived in Louisville alone, so every few months we would go down and spend time with her on the weekends. I actually didn't mind the drive or the time with her mom.

That year, we visited the week before December, and were on the way back when my ex asked me to stop at a K-Mart on the south edge of Columbus. It was snowy out and late on a Sunday evening. She didn't even buy much, she mostly just window shopped. But she did leave her purse in the shopping cart when she pushed it out of the way so we could leave. With all our money in it. Including our rent money.

When we went back to get it 20 minutes later, it was too late. The purse was gone. But for some reason, I was not upset about it. We argued constantly, but not about this for some reason. I just wasn't all that upset about it. I let our landlord know what happened, and worked out a plan to pay the rent as we went and make it up. No problem.

It was a plan I never needed to make, because God was just about to get involved. That Wednesday, John Avanzini was coming to a church on the very outskirts of Worthington, all but out in the country. I wanted to go and hear him, so that evening we packed up the kids and drove. Thing is, we only had enough gas to get there and a little less than halfway home. I just didn't let it bother me.

John Avanzini was amazing. He told about how he would go to the hospital to pray for people and the alarms would go off and nurses would be scrambling throughout the floor he was on. He explained how he got to know what his gifting was, and talked about how it was he first realized it when in Africa. Then came the end of the service.

Mr. Avanzini made a peculiar request; when the plate is passed, put something, anything, in it. If you are broke, put the pencil from the back of the pew in front of you into the plate, but put something in it. I told my ex to do it - in fact, I prayed that if God was to do anything to go through her, as I was already comfortable with the whole situation and knew what I believed.

After the service, I took our daughter to the atrium with the hopes I would get to meet Mr. Avanzini. And I did. I waited inside the front of the building as the crowd filtered out, then the pastors with the guests, then most of the staff. Finally, when the building was all but abandoned, my ex came out and simply asked to leave.

When we reached the car, she told me how she was talking to a woman who had been sitting near her after the service as they were both pregnant at the time. While they chatted, people kept coming up to her and saying, "I don't know why, but I am supposed to give you this." And there in the church parking lot inside the car, she pulled over $600 out of her pocket. We had a decent Christmas that year.

To the Atheist, I would say this; God usually shows up in people suits. He does most things through people. One of the things I would tell my Atheist friends is that for the believer, we occasionally actually hear from God. And yes, there are times when he actively heals someone or takes other action directly. The issue comes back to the randomness. God is incredibly fickle, and we have no way of knowing why, except He really likes to get us to do stuff for others.

On the other hand, i would remind you that there are plenty of times when someone suffers also through no fault of their own yet it is not the end of the story. As brilliant as Stephen Hawking was, he still lived in a wheelchair. No matter how rich and powerful you are, we will all go the way of John McCain and enter the grave one day. Everybody's mommy dies. Everyone's mommy dies. All of them.

So suffering, or more correctly the lack of relief of suffering is not an indicator of God's lack of mercy. Could God do more to alleviate suffering? It would seem so. There is literally a place in the New Testament where it says that Jesus simply healed the entire crowd of people that came to see him. Does Jesus love some Jewish people from 2,000 years ago more than you and me?

All I can do is put the cards on the table and say that

just because everyone of us do not get everyone on our wish list is no proof of God existence or goodness. This is exactly the same as it has been every Christmas of our lives since we were kids for the vast majority of us, and a poor indication that God doesn't love us/exist. Nevertheless I also have to say this; people who are only interested in today have lots more reason to panic than I do. If I end up being homeless it will not be the first time and I can deal with it.

I have had both good and bad from life, and I am not going to let that make me compromise what I am trying to do. Sooner or later I will find enough good to survive until I die. And then all this stuff gets left behind and will no longer matter to me at all. For all this life is made out to be, the overwhelming fact is life in this world is beyond all else is temporary. It's just for today.

And it's not like we are good at reading the tea leaves anyway. We are incredibly incapable of really planning anything for tomorrow. Companies such as Apple, which we pretend was brilliantly thought out, got lucky as often as they guessed right. They found a pattern for their devices that worked and made them popular and that is pretty smart but not like Einstein. Long ago, IBM was the big boy in the tech market but not any more. One day, Apple will be second rate and smaller like IBM, but I hope it is not for the next ten years when I will be using Apple products for my work.

We have limited ability to guess what we will need in the future beyond the basics. No one can guess if their spouse will die in an auto accident or if their house will be burnt to the ground in a spectacular conflagration. We assume, but when we pray we point to our needs today. Yet we are dealing with a being that can see all of time in the current. Of course we can know little of how such a being thinks.

We are unfortunately stuck with the God of sometimes. There is no other option, as there is no way to say that God never intervenes in human behavior. What we need is a way to find out, and for that we are limited to asking. So then, maybe we should ask. We might be shocked with the answer.

But the God of sometimes makes himself very clear. I wish to share with you the testimony I gave about this year (2018) on my personal Facebook page:

"Now that everything is settled, I get to tell my testimony how God took care of me this summer. It is a very good story.

I did not want to work at the University of Phoenix when I got the position there in technical support. I had worked a few other jobs over the years, including technical support for E4E taking support calls for Logitech products. I had figured out that call center positions are pretty much dead end jobs. In over 5 years at UOPX, I was interviewed one time total for a promotion, but when the managers have 50 or 100 or even more employees to choose from the odds are incredibly long. I have NEVER been promoted from the phones within a call center.

So over the winter, I had started several personal projects, both writing and music. Before that, I had spent years building up my skill and buying equipment. When I first started out, I had an Epiphone Les Paul Junior, the cheapest of the cheap electric guitars. It was so bad that Rocksmith would not register all the notes I was playing. My first bass was used, and the volume knob was mostly a dead spot.

But by last year, I was prepared to do some serious personal work. I had some music I was already working on that was shaping up, and several of the writing projects were ready to go. For years, I had been praying for God to get me out of UOPX, but last winter seemed to be perfect timing. I had saved up some money and would get my income tax return so I could live on that for a while as I completed my projects and job hunted. My prayers were answered in March when I was laid off. That alone blew me away.

Just when I was ready to get out, I almost blew it twice, but both times God stepped in and protected me. The first time was back in February of this year, I was driving home in the cold on my scooter and did not stop adequately enough for a Mesa cop at the corner of Broadway and Country Club, just a mile from my house. But it was a very cold night, about 45 degrees out, and the cop decided to have mercy and just give me a warning.

A few weeks later, and it had warmed up quite a bit as it does in Arizona. On the way to work I stopped at the Fry's Electronics in Tempe to pick up a cable. When I got back into traffic, I rear-ended a young lady at the light. I don't know why, but 99% of the time when the light turns green in Arizona, everyone rolls forward about 5 feet then slams on the brakes. I was not aware green means stop, but apparently it does in this state. I was not paying enough attention and I tapped her bumper with my scooter.

She had me pull back into the parking lot and called the police. She spoke with them for about 15 minutes, then suddenly decided I did not hurt anything and let me off and drove away. If I had gotten a ticket either time, I would not have had the money to take the summer off. But God was with me, and I got to save the hundreds a ticket would have cost me.

I used my time off to do all the work I had told God I would complete, Two books and two songs (one song needs fixed badly). Then I started other projects as well (this book is one of them). And I refused to take another call center job, and went after jobs I wanted. For about 3 months after I finished my projects I just waited to get a job and started on new things. Finally, I got a new job last week. It is not a call center, and it is a great place to work.

Things will be tight for the next few weeks but after that everything should return to normal. So God actually gave me my prayer requests, right down to the details. And He let me take off as much time as possible so I could be rested. I did not have to drive to work on my scooter in the summer heat a single time.

Not only that, but I took a forebearance on my student loans when I was laid off. I had one loan with a different lender that did not do consolidations with the Department of Education. But when my forebearance went through, they decided to place that loan with another servicer unbeknownst to me. Last week the loan servicer contacted me, and now my last loan is being taken over by my main loan servicer, so from here on I should only have one loan payment to make instead of two.

God has been very good to me this year. Thank you Jesus!!!!"

Why did God help me and not some others, like kids in the hospital with cancer? I can't say for sure - that's the unknown part. The answer would probably be complicated; part love for me, part my willingness to work on these projects, part my willingness to testify to it, part the effect all of this has on the different people, both those reading this and the family of the kid with cancer. And if you belong to God, from His viewpoint there is really no loss anyway. We believers and children all go from living here on earth to living in His house.

But this is where we are, the God maybe not so much of sometimes as the God of strange faithfulness. The God who intervenes based on all He sees and knows rather than what we see here in today. It may not be the best answer, but it seems the most accurate. Strangely, much of the good I have received has come to me since both my parents died. Yet here I am testifying that some things are very good and I want every one to know that I give glory to the Father for his blessings.

It's all so ethereal but very real this God of strange faithfulness. We should get to know Him better, and understand Him better. Drop the 30-point plan to get Him to obey our desires. Follow instead of lead, and see where He takes us. In a weird way, the answer is both always good and not so important as the travel we take to get us there.

Give it a try and see if the God of strange faithfulness will become the God of today for you the way He has for me.

PART TWO: TO BE MERE ANIMALS

CHAPTER SIX
DEATH BY HUBRIS

To the ancient Greeks, hubris was the root from which the entire bitter tree of disaster grows. Before one loves or hates, fears or trusts, one believes the view they hold of the world, and the objects in it, is more correct than all others. It is hubris that makes up the devil whispering evil in our ears, and to a good point they were absolutely correct. It is hubris that opens the door to error and destruction. It is the seed of all vices, and yet it remains poorly defined despite our desperate need to understand it. And of all the human depravities it is the only one that it intrinsic to every single human. We all have the individual sins we love, but every single human has hubris in their heart.

The basic meaning of the word is simple: The conviction one's own understanding is superior to that of others. As a clinical description, this is fine, though superficial. To understand hubris it is necessary to understand the source of hubris. That is a deeper and more detailed mechanism. It all starts with consciousness.

Without consciousness there can be no hubris. Self-awareness is the bedrock hubris is built on. A mountain lion may starve to death in winter if it cannot find food in the harsh environment, and the fish who does not hide well enough in the reef may get eaten. But they instinctively live in the environments they are proficient for, so an angelfish would no more try to live in a tree than a mountain lion would try to live at the bottom of the Mediterranean.

Humans are different. All members of homo sapiens who do not have physical impairment to the brain (and many who do) are aware of their own existence and their own thoughts. And we are aware of ourselves in the environment. We are the only beings on the planet that think in terms of "desert" or "forest" or "nuclear physics" or "Lindsey Lohan".

Beyond this, we are the only creatures who make wide scale adjustments to the different environments to make them more secure, comfortable, and livable. A tiny percentage of animals do something similar, but only based on instinct. Birds build nests, but not skyscrapers. Beavers build dams, but not highways from Salt Lake City to Las Vegas.

The normal things we point to as setting humans apart from the animals can be described more succinctly as "The abilities necessary to intentionally organize social groups to manipulate and exploit the environment". But with that comes the curse of hubris. Not only is it common for individuals to see to their own needs before others (greed), but hubris goes beyond just this.

In order to successfully manipulate and exploit the environment we need to be able to generally agree on what the terms "desert" and "forest" mean. We do this by building mental pictures of both physical and non-physical things. But we have this thing in our brains that we do not bring data in the same way. The word "jungle" looks different to the farmer in India than it did to the artists of The Jungle Book.

We colorize things. We imagine things. We consider the non-physical and physical realities of the universe with the same general processes and blend them together. We learn from our elders and our peers and our experiences, and all this combined creates a mental lens we see the world through. This lens becomes a wide screen that helps us both recognize the things we see as good and ignore or resist that which we see as evil.

But our lenses don't work right. Left on our own, the vast majority of the world rises only to the level of petty thieves; lacking the intensity to commit great good or evil. Only those at the edges of the bell curves become Mother Theresa or Stalin. Most stop caring when their bellies are full. And throughout history this appears to be the baseline of who we are as creatures. The empire that replaced the previous was just like it, only differing in language, currency, and idols.

The problem arises because we can only communicate physically. We have no way to share the full mental landscape we build in our minds with others. Physical communication, even in our time, is a tedious, limited endeavor. Further, the mediums and signals available are pathetically simple, barely more advanced than our stone age ancestors.

The result is one of being trapped in our own minds.

And, since everything we input, from the fact we survived a day to the news we watch reinforces our own view as being fundamentally correct and viable for all of human endeavor. That special set of skills which gives us our consciousness also gives us the curse of hubris. It is the point of the fall in the book of Genesis; when Adam and Eve ate of the forbidden fruit, they saw differently. And that limited, slightly warped seeing that is filtered through our own understanding is the mechanism of hubris.

The Greeks, despite the carefully considered look at the individual understanding of hubris as a personal issue, they had a hard time pointing it out regularly on a small scale. This is also a matter of human social habit, because while we consider individuals at times as narcissists, hubris really raises its ugly head in public debate and activity.

In The Histories by Thucydides , hubris takes a toll on both sides. Each side had the ability to walk away and consolidate their position, bide their time and try to tip the scales in their favor, but each failed in turn. Those involved in the conflict could not correctly measure their strategic position nor the accurate likelihood of success or failure. Their own presuppositions and prejudices cooked their judgment in a pot full of emotions. A study of the Histories is a study in hubris, so let's take a closer look.

The Spartans were the first to make an error. Quite by accident they sacrificed their most brilliant general in a story reminiscent of the fate of German generals in WWII, and for largely the same reason…overconfidence and indifference.

At the beginning of the conflict, Athens had the strategic advantage. Surrounded by the Mediterranean, they had developed a large, experienced fleet that dominated the sea. Further, they had a defensive plan that protected both the city and the nearby port from land attack with a huge wall that was basically un-scalable. There was no way to cut off the connection to the sea.

Being the head of an empire, Athens had through tribute and trade built an extensive reserve with which they could buy whatever supplies they needed. But more than anything else they had one particular ace up their sleeve - they did not rely on the local farms for all their food. They had allies in northern Greece who could supply them with grain from their abundant harvests.

In response, a commander named Brasidas gathered up some 700 troops and 1000 mercenaries for a campaign in Thrace in 430 BC. He was a brilliant general, cutting a swath through enemy territory that threatened to cut off the Athenian food supply. He defeated an Athenian attack on Megara, then slashed his way through Thessaly to Macedonia.

And here, it all started to fall apart. Perdiccas, king of Macedonia, was brilliant at playing the part of Mussolini. He wanted Brasidas to succeed…as long as he could gain from it without risking too much. In other words, he would not commit, though much like the latter, would be willing to ride in on his white horse as victorious king once the battle ended.

That meant Brasidas was on his own with a small force of loyal troops and another small force that was only as loyal as the pay was regular. So Brasidas changed tactics, conducting a political blitz of persuading the nearby cities to change allegiance. This was a startling success, and such a threat to the Athenians that Thucydides himself was sent with a force to stabilize the situation, and he successfully defended Eion from the Spartans.

The situation was so dire the next year, in 423 BC, the Athenians negotiated a truce. Sparta sat on the verge of victory, and responded to their great fortune by…doing nothing. Nothing at all. And here, we have the first intentionally recorded attack of social hubris in the most baffling version, antipathy.

For some bizarre reason, the Spartans seemed committed to refusing to wrap their minds around the strategic situation. Athens did everything but crawl to indicate their desperation yet the Spartans never seemed to notice in the slightest. It was so bad that two days after the truce began the city of Scione also flipped to the Spartans, followed by Mende. Athens immediately demanded the return of Scione, which Brasidas refused. The situation was absolutely critical, and the future of Athens hung in the balance. The Battle of Britain never came anywhere near such a razor edge.

While the truce was on, Brasidas joined forces with Perdiccas to defeat Arrhabaeus, king of the Lyncesti. But Perdiccas ran at the approach of a force of turncoat Illyrians however Brasidas managed to save his smaller force. But it was all to be for naught, because for whatever reason the Spartans never sent reinforcements. Like Rommel in North Africa, his forces were bled out slowly and never received the support they needed.

So what was it the Spartan leaders did not get? They had the larger army, and could easily spare another couple thousand troops. Brasidas marched his troops to the theatre, so any reinforcements could have done that as well. Athens could not afford to send an expedition to cut the reinforcements off, they only had the manpower to make one last desperate try at stabilizing the situation, and if it failed they would be forced to surrender.

One of the signs of hubris is conceit, the belief your opponent does not have the capability to be victorious. It has been the bugaboo of military leadership ever since the first of our ancestors began to make clubs and spears and use them on each other. Certainly, the Spartans had to see the golden opportunity that Brasidas kicked open for them. Maybe they believed the silly idea that leadership was to manpower as 10 is to 1, or the ignorant maxim that morale is to numbers as 10 is to 1.

I do not wish to underestimate the effect of morale, but morale is based on a variety of factors. Training, loyalty, tactics and quality of equipment all feed into the level of morale of a fighting force as much as leadership. Troops need effective weapons and gear; tactics that give them an opportunity of being successful; and leadership that is intelligent and observant enough to maneuver those forces into position to be able to be successful.

After the embarrassment of the trail of broken down tanks Germany faced in the annexation of Austria in March of 1938, there was little reason to believe the strategy of blitzkrieg would actually work. But with years of training, new equipment, and adoption of the lessons learned from the experience, the Germans started an incredible run of military victories only eighteen months later.

The Italians had already invaded Ethiopia well prior to Hitler being able to have enough troops to defend the Ruhr in an emergency. At the time of the invasion in 1935, the Italians had decent aircraft and tanks, and a small but completely modern fleet. Yet things went in a different direction in Italy. Development and production stagnated. Equipment aged, Ethiopia became a slow burn, and Il Duce never even tried to develop the heavy steel industry necessary to make modern tanks.

By the time the war started, morale was low, weapons outdated, and the navy could not venture into open seas because they could not realistically count on any air support at all once out of range of the land based antiaircraft guns at the ports. The German military, little more than a joke when Ethiopia was invaded, romped across Europe, suffering a total of only about 84,000 casualties through the end of 1940. There were over 51,000 casualties at the Battle of Gettysburg alone, just to provide some reference. In that time frame, the Italian armies were pushed back across their own borders not only in Southern France in 1940, but in Greece in 1941 as well.

The English easily pushed the Italian forces out of East Africa, and they were never militarily important thereafter. And everyone and their kid brother should have been able to see it coming, which was exactly why Hitler was appeased at Munich while Mussolini was ignored a little more every day by the major players of the approaching storm. This misreading of reality, of overestimating your realistic capabilities is a central part of hubris. It feeds upon the inflated ego.

This misreading of actual capability to perceived capability has been the downfall of empires from time immemorial. And it was some strange form of this disease that befell the Spartans at just the worst time. The next year, the truce ended, and the Athenians were ready. The fleet was sent, which stabilized the situation while fresh forces were sent ashore. Brasidas took advantage of the slow moving troops and managed to break down the much larger forces. The problem was, when you go against a much larger force at close range, you put yourself in considerable danger. It was a pyrrhic victory, of which Brasidas himself was a casualty.

Without leadership, reinforcements, or allies, the threat, just recently at critical stage, now melted away. Just by luck, the Athenians had done barely enough. But it was really the luck of the Spartans which ran out, after rolling the dice once too often. Let this be a lesson to you; all good things come to an end, and if you will not reason correctly, your Waterloo may be just around the corner.

When you rely on luck to supplement your skill by making unreasonably long odds for yourself, those odds eventually turn against you. Sparta would now endure some bad luck of their own, long overdue. The Athenians decided to go on the offensive, and chose the target wisely if not the rest; they took aim at Sicily, in particular Syracuse. They also came to the assistance of the Acarnanians. Demosthenes proved a failure in Acarnania at first, but elsewhere victory bloomed.

Eventually Demosthenes managed a victory and to return home. The Athenians made definite progress in Sicily, controlling the straight of Messina and surrounding islands before peace was declared. But by sheer luck, they landed a small force on a small peninsula in the southwest of the Peloponnese called Pylos. At first it looked like a disaster, but with a narrow front it proved impossible to assault frontally. To outmaneuver the garrison, the Spartans occupied the island to the south called Sphacteria. That was an error. The Athenian fleet quickly isolated them, and when the Spartans were forced to surrender, that part of the war was over, in 421 BC. In a little more than a year, Sparta went from the verge of success to the hollow of defeat.

However, this turned out only to be a prelude to the main spectacle. The central act of hubris plays out in Book VI when the Athenians decide to invade Sicily.

After only six years of general peace, much of the damage done to the Athenians was repaired, at least financially and locally. But the war had apparently not taught the Athenians the correct lesson, so they would learn it one more time before disaster struck. In 418 BC, the Athenians joined the Arcadians to try to take Tegea, which would have ended the Spartan ability to wage war. Instead, they suffered another defeat. Then, three more years of silence.

But the tantalizing success of Sicily lingered. And after they were asked to leave by the united leaders of the Island, Syracuse worked to expand it's power. As a result, Egesta sent ambassadors to Athens requesting assistance. That was all it took to get visions of empire dancing in Athenian heads. For whatever fantastical reason, the Athenians thought they could conquer this island that was equal to about 18% or so of all Greece.

Upon hearing how difficult the invasion would be as described by the general Nicias the Athenians are not discouraged, but rather decide to go all in, massively expanding the expeditionary force to overwhelming proportions. It was a complete disaster. They could find all but no allies to work with, and never really seriously tried to help the Egestaeans. Instead, they eventually tried what everyone thought they were really going to do; conquer Syracuse. They nearly win the first battle, but that is often the way overstretch feels, like the goal is just beyond the fingertips.

The Athenians retreat to recoup and resupply, but that gives Syracuse the same opportunity. And the Syracuse sent for assistance from Sparta. They are informed by the Athenian general Alcibiades that Athens has stars in it's eyes; once Sicily fell, Italy proper was next, then eventually Carthage itself. How they could do this is unfathomable, considering they did not have the manpower to conquer their own neighbors.

This is the other part of hubris that is so surprisingly strong; the tendency of greediness. Not just underestimating your opponent, but vastly overestimating your own powers. Of going beyond exploiting an opportunity to literally seeing imaginary ones. This reaching is probably the craziest part of hubris. And generally, they reaching is by miles, encouraged in modern society by sloganeering such as "you can be anything you want to be", one of the silliest statements of all time. It is patently untrue. A 5 foot tall woman in a wheelchair cannot be an NBA player.

After they reorganize, the Athenians have some success. Some groups join with the Athenians as they begin to taste success. Back home, however, they make another critical error; they start to conduct raids in the Peloponnesus, and the war flames back up again. And Nicias makes a crucial misstep at this point, having started a wall to isolate the land side of Syracuse, he does not complete it. The Syracuse build their own counter wall, providing an access channel that prevents the Athenians from isolating them from the rest of the island.

Both sides receive reinforcements, but the Syracusian additions are larger, and used wisely. Slowly the tide turns. The invading force is not holding its own very well, and small defeats on land and sea start to cripple operations and crush morale. A nighttime attack on the Syracuse lines is a failure, adding to the weight of the situation. Unlike Greece, the really high mountainous parts of Sicily were located in the northern interior. Along much of the outer edges of the islands the land is more open, made of rolling hills rather than the rugged terrain of the homeland.

And the troops of Syracuse had horses, as did most of the rest of the island. The Athenian allies had some, but not enough, and the hoplites did not know how to deal with them. Adequate tactics and strategies were never implemented. So combined forces of horses and troops slowly went from poor defenders to coordinated strike forces.

Suddenly it was over. Most of the fleet was lost, and when the troops on land collapsed they did so completely, unable to bear up under the combined assault of the Syracuse forces. The rest is history.

The book ends here, and many believe the author dies at this point. But we do know what happens after the book ends. At first, Athens bounces back, rebuilding the fleet and restoring balance. And then again the people of Athens make a critical mistake.

During the Battle of Arginusae part of the Athenian fleet was lost due to bad weather. It was certainly a tragedy, but natural disasters are not new and can interfere in military operations just like any other activity. The people of Athens should have been able to accept the losses as a part of the natural cost of having a large fleet that could dominate the Adriatic in time of war.

Instead, the Athenians responded in an overwhelmingly emotional manner. The response to the casualties was to demand the punishment of the Athenian naval commanders. Six were eventually put to death.

Now the war turned for the last time; by crippling their leadership they allowed the Spartans naval commander Lysander to outmaneuver and defeat the Athenian fleet. Facing starvation, Athens surrendered in 404 BC.

Now that I have painted as detailed a picture of hubris we need to view it in the current sociopolitical environment. It does not involve military force much these days, but it is still every bit the psychic poison it always was. Long before there is a single failure, hubris colors every thought and every decision of the sufferer.

Today, hubris is attached to technology. Humans have this annoying habit of pretending we are far more in control of the world than we really are, and our technology is proof of this in our minds. The New Atheist movement sees themselves as supporting science versus primitive belief, but this is not reality. It allows them to ignore the four legs of human understanding, which I mentioned earlier.

But hubris becomes a trap; it mineralizes the emotional life of the user. The reason the New Atheists are so evangelical is because it stokes their ego to scold others into agreement, as if submission of others validates their views. There is no space for understanding, much less compromise. The assault made on Masterpiece Cake Shop is but a symptom of the disease. So are the Twitter mobs, the Antifa movement, the anger of feminist theology, the frustration of the media over the election of Donald Trump.

That emotional cage keeps the person contained therein from the truth. There is no space for admitting the tax cuts under Trump have improved the economy. No space for limits on emotional appeals. It leads to no-borders policies, even though America simply cannot adopt 7.6 billion people, and most would not be interested anyway. Being self-righteous becomes a way of life, over which the individual is unwilling to deflate their ego enough to listen to reason - even though the belief in reason was the base of the psychological structure that now traps the victim.

Our control of the world is not nearly as great as we believe. I have been job hunting over the last few months, and there is very little about the process I have control over. All I can do is tell the interviewer how what I have been doing will help me contribute in the position I have applied for. But showing up and talking and wearing a suit and not smelling bad is all I can do.

I have no control over the quality of the other applicants. I have no real control over whether the person believes my personality will mesh with the other members of the team. I can't even fully persuade them that I am as competent as I am. All I can do is give the understanding of who I am and what I can do.

In response, we listen to the Secret, that all we want can be ours if we just desire it bad enough. This is silly. The environment in which you work limits your ability, which is why astronauts do not remove their helmets outside the capsule. We believe, however, so we fail to plan and fail to work, which keeps us from getting as far we can.

But here lies the real message the Ancients were trying to convey to us; tragedy is for losers. True, cancer sucks, and being short or deformed or mentally challenged are the cards we are given and cannot change. Yes, we have little power against hurricanes and meteors. So whence comes all our ego?

That is the part they wanted to warn us about. Earthquakes and droughts are bad enough without us considering ourselves masters of the universe. What the Greeks and others meant by tragedy we today would call "drama". And drama, my friend, is for losers. The emotionalism, the suffocating sense of self importance, the unchecked demand to be not just treated equally but liked and agreed with, that is tragedy. Tragedy of the highest kind, tragedy noticed by the gods themselves.

This tragedy, this playing out of the drama - that is the true tragedy of life. We accept the idea that living on the coast may mean the occasional hurricane. That living in the north may lead to freezing to death. That scratching out a living inland from the dirt may depend on the summer rains. We do our best to mitigate our chances and do our best. But it's quite another thing to make an expedition to the north pole wearing a polo shirt and sandals since you are going in the summertime.

Real tragedy involves our temporary insanity, the way we forget our limitations and weaknesses for things that seems so easy yet turn out so hard. It is a normal soul lead by a demonic amount of arrogance, unable to see his own feet for his superiority. I once had a buffoon sit down with me at a Bible study and swear he had never lied in his life, and demand I he prove he had, despite the fact I knew nothing about him but his name. I laughed at him, as that was all I could do, and only had one lie to go by. But this is all you can do, and hope he never takes over his dad's business, for he would be sure to run it into the ground in flames. But you don't have to personally destruct to fail. You can always throw your neighbor under the bus instead.

Let me give you a football analogy from the 2018 regular season if I may. For this example I would like to discuss the Pittsburgh Steelers with you. At the start of the season, they were considered one of the top contenders to make the Super Bowl. They had several stars on offense, and the defense was young but improving despite some setbacks in previous years. Then, hubris happened.

When you are incredibly talented, and have worked hard to perfect your skill, it is human nature to slack off a little. We recognize the "Super Bowl hangover", as winners tend to struggle the following year, as the distractions of flattery and attention pulls them away from the habits that make them winners and their egos lead them to believe they are better than others by nature rather than effort.

So when the season started, the players on the Steelers had done enough to look decent. But Ben Roethlisberger is a champion quarterback, so if he goes a little easy it can be hard to spot and even harder to pressure him to push himself. And when you are Antonio Brown, one of the top wide receivers in the NFL – the type of player who can end your professional career early as a defensive back, it's a little hard to call him out, too. The best running back over the last few years, Le'veon Bell, can decide to sit out so he can be paid the kind of money that shows the Steeler's value of him and be OK. He has cash on hand already. But here is the thing; it's perfectly possible to do very well and still fail.

Right now, December 26, 2018 Antonio Brown has almost 1,300 receiving yards, and two more touchdowns than the next receiver. He is literally averaging one per game. And Big Ben has more yardage than anyone else, even Patrick Mahomes. Those offensive players are doing well for themselves all but one thing; they are about to miss the playoffs altogether.

How you personally are doing in your life is absolutely no indication of how your team is doing. It is completely possible for every single person reading this to book to be doing quite well in your personal lives, and yet we are still likely to lose the war. Likely to lose the war. Not some slight percentage, but likely, more inclined to happen than not happen. Hubris is so hard to defeat because it is a self-contained cocoon of me, all day long.

What makes tragedy what it is comes from the destruction it causes to real potential. History is littered with stories of but for this one mistake, and humans have committed countless unknown personal tragedies as well. Yet the Ancients are insistent that tragedy is for losers, for the wise listen and learn and measure before they swing the axe even once. "You must act now!" is a sales pitch, not a way of life.

Some find the Kardashians and other reality stars fascinating. And there is a little good mixed in with the bad if truth be told. But that addiction to drama, that is the poor lot of too many of us, for here in the real world, the story does not end with everyone going back to their middle-class homes to live happily ever after until the next dust up. Her in the real world it leads to broken homes and broken children and a broken society. It leads to poverty and despair and misery the measure of which is totally unnecessary. It leads to loneliness and heartbreak and mental breakdown, anger and violence and hatred for those who have committed only imaginary crimes.

Drama may be, with video games and Social Justice, among the last few approved activities of the Hard Left and New Atheism, but I can say one thing about these activities - they are truly for losers. And losers they be.

CHAPTER SEVEN
THE BLIND LEADING THE BLIND

When I was in high school, it was a right of passage to get a part-time job or at least to do certain work to make extra money. I worked at my uncle's gas station and shoveled snow in the winter and horse manure in the spring which the neighbors used in their gardens. My best friend's girlfriend did what millions of teenagers used to do; she got a job in fast food. She made enough money to buy her own car, in fact. I also later worked in the industry myself right after school.

Things have certainly changed. Now fast food restaurants are largely filled with college students and Hispanics who lack other skills. Actual teenagers face an uphill battle to get any of these positions now. Sure, companies like Chick-Fil-A and In-N-Out Burger still hire college students, but those are 22-year-olds, not 16-year-olds.

What the Hard Left will never truly entertain in a serious manner is the fact that every change in a society has opportunity costs attached to it. In the fast food industry the opportunity cost of illegal immigration is the sacrifice of providing a way for teenagers to enter the job market - the exact reason they have to take jobs in fast food industries while in college in the first place.

But even worse is the results of that education, which leaves a huge percentage (at least a plurality) unready for a job even after they graduate college, as they are still unprepared for the positions that are available. There is an opportunity cost to spending four years learning about the leftist proclivities of your professors; you don't learn any actual skills that way.

Giving amnesty to those currently illegally living in America comes with opportunity costs as well. The first one is the already mentioned – the damage you do to the future of your own children. But there is another one as well, as others who might be deterred from illegally coming to America will now be encouraged to do so, in the hopes that history will repeat itself and they too would eventually receive amnesty.

The Hard Left claims these are jobs that "Americans won't do" but this is fraudulent on its face. Americans have been doing just those kinds of jobs for hundreds of years. There is even a TV show called "Dirty Jobs" by Mike Rowe. The left does not make arguments, merely suppositions based on worldview.

But there is another, even greater opportunity cost that no one is mentioning, the growing undercurrent of disrespect for American institutions and values. The Hard Left of today's politics are perfectly fine with this removal of value and process. Don't like the current White House occupant? Drum him out of office. Don't like federal immigration laws? Pass your own sanctuary laws and undercut federal power. Don't like the opinions of others? Reject free speech. Can't get laws passed according to the constitution? Just use your phone and pen to write your own, bypassing the legal procedures of congress as prescribed in the constitution.

It is on the opportunity costs of their policies that the Hard Left totally loses the argument, because they are totally unwilling to be honest about them. I would go as far as to say I would never believe any of the numbers the left spews on any subject, scientific or economic. They are famous for fudging numbers if not outright lying, and use those imaginary numbers to manipulate others.

Let me give you a clear and obvious example proving beyond the shadow of a doubt how dishonest the Hard Left is about opportunity costs. They claim that wages have not risen in real terms since the 1970's and this is the consequence of conservative policies. In truth it is no such thing. It was really the opportunity costs of ensuring blacks and women were incorporated into the workforce.

Let me state here that I absolutely do not want the opportunities for anyone to be limited. In fact, there is a crowd of fellow conservatives who have become successful in the public sphere who are black or women, and I celebrate them. I even look up to a couple. But this does not mean we get to do bad math and lie just because we favor the results.

Of course salaries have not risen much over inflation during this time. We added millions of workers to the workforce over a short period of time between 1960 and 1980. That means the salaries available to businesses to pay workers had to be spread out across millions of extra people, which naturally would depress wages overall. The real result of this is the inability for most families to get by on one salary.

That means most women have to work, whether they want to or not. The vast majority do not seem to mind, but there is still an opportunity cost of no longer having a choice - even for women, the only choice is work or go without. Only in the twisted minds of the Hard Left is this the best outcome available.

The complaint of the Hard Left is that these new workers, lacking skills and experience, should still be paid the same as the workers already providing economic value to the company. They imagined that if the average salary was 35k, then everybody added to the economy should also make the same. This is nothing more than the worst kind of magical thinking possible, and the Hard Left uses it constantly as a battering ram against conservatives despite the whole argument being mere fallacy.

In fact, due to the 25 years of all but unbroken growth and prosperity we did eventually absorb the vast majority of newcomers into the workforce including immigrants. But in order for salaries to rise, the process has to come to an end eventually. But not in the illogical mind of the left. No, they want to make something close to 20 million more illegal immigrants legal citizens. So let's do some math, because math is true and everyone a liar.

Even if illegal immigrants do contribute 11 billion dollars to the economy, that is spread out across 10 million plus people. So each one only contributes 11 thousand dollars. Yet the 330 million or so citizens have an economy of about 19 trillion, well over $57,000 each. The contributions of illegals to the economy is incredibly inadequate to make amnesty a good argument economically.

The Hard Left continues the magical thinking by believing that if we would just make them citizens, they would magically gain marketable skills and experience through some sort of unknown absorption. But even if that was true, and their contribution tripled - tripled, mind you - to 30 thousand dollars instantaneously, they would still be an incredible drag on the economy. And their effect on spreading out salaries and locking out others from entry level jobs would still be unsolved.

This is the crux of the problem when it comes to the Hard Left; good or bad, they simply will not come clean when it comes to the math. And if they are willing to so openly and blatantly lie to you about one subject, they will lie to you about any subject. That is exactly what we find, a pattern of consistent lying about all subjects, big and small, and always and consistently when it comes to anything regarding economics.

The reason for this is experience bias. The Hard left does not actually believe in any sort of unified form of economics. They support "free trade" and the high taxes and social costs it creates, then blame business leaders for doing what is best for their companies and moving to lower cost workforces. They think the American economy will always be bountiful just because, and seem to believe entrepreneurs and business leaders are running their companies as a hobby, complaining about high compensation for those individuals yet never realizing everyone in a company from top to bottom are paid out of those very profits the company is making.

It is hard to understand why anyone in the whole world believes in a bit of this nonsense, yet billions of people do, for no good reason at all. If there is no other evidence available, the willingness of people to follow economic systems that make no sense proves beyond a shadow of a doubt how little a huge number of our fellow human beings are actually attached to reason and logic.

The only thing seen by the Hard Left and the New Atheism is the story they have adopted from the Soviets or worldwide oppression by capitalist overlords. This is insufficient to see the world the way it really is. And the sterile way they see the world allows no space for anything they do not understand.

I have to be honest with you; I see Providence in absolutely everything that is happening in the world today. I have personally had an incredibly blessed year and many of the things that have happened have made these books possible. But even on a national level I see Providence on a much wider scale in the U.S. and the West.

Technologically, we are in just the place we need to be in order to maintain our energy self sufficiency through fracking. We really don't need to go for all these crazy social and economic ideas, because God is giving us a second chance at doing this right, holding out grace to us as long as possible. Truth is we put ourselves in a hard spot with the housing meltdown. Everyone wants to put the blame on crooked bankers but won't take responsibility for being crooked borrowers. Yet here we are with a second chance to do the right thing.

Of course God is allowing the Muslims to rise again. He prefers to allow the wicked rule rather than the rebellious. There is a spiritual principle that rebelliousness draws the attention of the evil who manipulate the rebellious. Further, the Muslims have a point about the nature of Western civilization. The individualism at the core of our institutions and values has been completely demolished, transformed from the healthy provision of the ability of every person to respond to life in a responsible way to nothing more than a sickly self-indulgence that has no ethos at all.

Interestingly enough, the vast majority of people who are doing anything to resist the Muslim surge are Christians and Hindus who clearly see the danger in Muslim dominance of nations. No country currently controlled by Muslims provide anything close to the rights offered in Westernized nations. Providence leads those of faith to be the main group to reject Islam as an equal and fellow-traveller of religiousness.

China likewise is reaching the maximum extent of it's power, and will slowly fall over the next few decades just like other low-fertility nations. Providence has determined that China and its communism will never rule the world, thus we are eventually to be free of that as well. It is also true that most of Latin America seems to be coming around to understanding how markets work, slowly and painfully as it is, and moving to the right as well. Ultimately, China will lack the economic power to provide the kind of influence to Latin America they have in parts of the Middle East and Africa. Even there, the pumping of billions of dollars into the continent by China may not be sustainable for much longer. It also turns out the terms of Chinese loans are becoming problematic to the nations borrowing from the Chinese.

And with medical technology beginning to seriously turn its attention to gestating humans in artificial wombs there may be a saving grace available to us just in time for the population crunch we are facing. Perhaps parts of Europe will slowly become Muslim Majority but not fast enough to delay other nations using medical technology to bolster their populations before it is too late.

In all of this there is the ultimate Providence of our

situation; we literally have only two issues which we need to overcome; the selfishness that is driving down our fertility rates and destroying our civilization, and our completely inadequate response to Islam. That's it. If we would just stop and humble ourselves and come to terms with reality we could have a relatively easy time of it. Our enemies are not that powerful, and also have limitations that give us hope for victory.

Through our circumstances God's Providence is literally spelling it out for us; if we would repent and give access to ourselves over to the good of our people and the world, we would have literally no problem overcoming what could turn out to be either an insurmountable mountain or minor speed bump, and which it becomes is entirely our choice. The whole thing is so ridiculously clear that the only thing God hasn't done is to be to literally make an infomercial and force us to watch it on YouTube.

If you enjoy and have adopted the Absurdist philosophy, I present to you the greatest absurdity in the history of all mankind; if we would just come to a compromise about the utility of families and children to the creation of the future and adopt those ideas as a society we could easily do everything needed to secure the future of the planet. The entire planet. Yet this simple solution is the very thing we refuse to do, as we choose to burn the future of our families to the ground in order that we may have an iPhone and a 4K TV.

If that is not absurd I do not know what is. And every single, last drop of that absurdity is due to those who are blind to every real virtue, living in their own little world truly uncaring about their fellow human beings in any meaningful way. Unless the person is one of the LGBTQ alphabet, whom they support unequivocally for no other reason than to oppress their imaginary enemies and crow about their self-righteousness. This nonsense leads to the most shallow and useless life possible.

It bothers them not one whit about human suffering anywhere in the world, and it will literally take bombs in their own neighborhoods before they will ever admit there is an issue with Islam, and they will still not do the right thing, for those who are brainwashed are incapable of believing anything they see with their own eyes. Instead, they will continue to insist that terrorism is the result of Western oppression and no a resurgent Islam that is following in the footsteps their forefathers marched twice. They are most blind who are so merely because they will not open their eyes.

Ergo, those on the Hard Left and among the New Atheists are the most blind of all.

CHAPTER EIGHT
THE VALUE OF NOTHING

There are values, things that one can think of as wrong as right, then there are the physical things you place value on. They are not necessarily the same things, although they can be. Normally there is a lot of overlap. The difference is what you work towards versus what you may express about a certain moral subject. So here I am not so much interested in what the "values" of the Hard Left may or may not be but rather what they value.

The thing valued above all other things by American leftists is power. They value power because the postmodernist core belief that the struggle for power is the central basis for all human activity. The accumulation of power then becomes the ultimate goal of the left. This leads to some damaging activities and public engagement that has warped not only people's views of life, but have proven to be horrendously damaging to everyday people's activity.

One of the most indicative examples of how the

Hard Left value power over the rights of individual citizens can be seen in the battles over those very individual rights. For the Hard Left, the issues one of gaining power over their enemies, not to seek a place at the table for everyone as they regularly suggest.

This tendency can be seen in the ruling of the Supreme Court in the masterpiece cake shop case. Here, there are two different parts to the ruling you need to pay attention to if you wish to understand it. However the facts of the case make both the beliefs and practices of the Hard Left concerning Christianity very clear.

The view of the hard left concerning the nature of Christianity as it was actually made part of the decision through the statements made by the Colorado Civil Rights Commission. The commission made it totally clear they placed absolutely no value on the Christian beliefs of the baker. Instead, keeping to their beliefs that all human interactions are about power, they saw the baker as using his Christian belief to discriminate.

Placing no value on the beliefs of the bakery owner the commission ruled on behalf of the plaintiffs not because any real damage had been done to them but as members of a group "lacking power" they deserved to have power over the bakery owner. This clear example of the exercise of the political power of the Hard Left and the New Atheists reveals the one critical mistake in their thinking.

For most of those on the Hard Left, the guarantee of the rights of the Constitution only apply to some people. They see the Constitution as protecting the poor, minorities, people of certain sexual proclivities and any other group they consider oppressed. In practice those on the Hard Left seek to gather together these oppressed groups and use the levers of power including the courts to consolidate power through those groups unto themselves.

This is a complete and utter twisting of both the spirit and letter of the law and understanding of the Constitution. The Constitution was not a document designed to protect the little guy. The Constitution was not designed just to protect the minority or the weak. It was designed specifically and intentionally to protect all of us. All of us. *All of us*.

That means the Constitution was designed to protect the rights of the owner of the bakery and his Christian beliefs **just as much** as the rights of gays. And when the Constitution is used to only protects some of us rather than for its stated goal of protecting all of us then the validity of our institutions are damaged if not destroyed. Credibility is lost not just for those wielding the power of the state but also the mechanisms through which they wield that power.

It is telling that the postmodernists and the Hard Left are willing to misuse power this way. We can infer from this that those on the left not only lack respect for those holding any type of traditional view on social issues but that they also fully intend to exercise control over those holding these traditional views, and also that they are true believers who believe that they are right and completely justified in doing so.

These practices extend beyond merely using the courts to enforce their exercising the power over others but extend into the public sphere where shaming, threatening, and occasionally physical violence is used to try to control their opponents. Together these acts paint a picture of the movement not constrained by the mores of a civil society as they attempt to gain the thing they value the most; power.

Those on the Hard Left base their right to exercise this type of power on their belief it is their responsibility to drag us into their Brave New World kicking and screaming, or at least through the bars of a prison camp. They call themselves progressives because they see themselves as actually possessing the intellectual key to social and technological advancement. They see those that resist them as backwards and parochial, not fit for anything other than manual labor and social control just as in Sir Thomas More's Utopia. The Hard Left see themselves as keepers of the flame just as portrayed in Utopia.

This toxic mix of ideology and political practice is what makes the Hard Left so dangerous. They really do feel justified in doing what ever it takes to make sure the social and technological progress they value above all else continues. And because they believe these changes to be so critically important to the future of humanity they feel fully justified in putting people in cages, or if necessary in front of a firing squad.

This is the kind of sickness that ends up causing people who've grown up in one of the most freest periods in human history to quote Stalin, one of the bloodiest dictators in history, that sometimes one must break some eggs to make an omelet. Only those are not eggs they are people, people that those on the left have murdered for over 100 years. From the concentration camps to the gulags to the killing fields of Cambodia to China today those are people we are talking about.

This is the real danger posed by those on the Hard Left. Even today in one of the freest the periods of human history we can clearly see that the power of the police state as supported by the left has not been defeated but only blunted in it's power. The social control we currently see seeping into our business environment and our educational environment and even into our ability just to express ourselves as citizens is not the first step to freedom, it is the first step to the police state.

Yes, there are plenty on the left who are currently for vehemently and violently against law enforcement, and this is been seen both in acts of violence towards the police and in resistance to agencies such as ICE. But we know how this story plays out; it is not that the Hard Left are against the police, they were only against the police they do not control. And when in complete control, they will become the guards at the camp.

Do not allow yourself to be fooled into believing that one day those on the left are simply going to do away with law enforcement. If you want to know what those who consider themselves anarchists really want for society don't bother imagining some magical peace-loving society in which the police are not needed. No, if you want to see what they really want for you and yours you should imagine the Cultural Revolution in China for that is the power they seek. They do not wish to do away with the police but rather to supplant them just as their ancestors the SS did in Germany so long ago.

There is nothing innocent in the way the Hard Left and the New Atheists view power. It is their ultimate goal in controlling society and punishing their enemies. It is a tool to be used in the creation of their bright shiny Star Trek future, and they intend to weld it just as ruthlessly and murderously as their ancestors did.

This battle against the oppression of the left has become the central theme of not just politics here in

America, but literally around the world. And it does much to explain the rise of President Trump and other leaders such as Victor Orban in Hungary. At its core it is a simple dichotomy; why would I or anyone else vote for someone who would put us in a concentration camp for practicing our Christian faith? Why should I vote for someone who would destroy my future for discussing the issues I am bringing up in this very book?

The Hard Left may try to deny that they have any such anti-Christian sentiments, but the left has been bullying the church for decades, literally decades. They dismiss traditional practices and beliefs as if they have not been part of the church's teaching for two millennia. They misquote and twist Scripture and use their mangled version to browbeat and shame Christian opponents all the while not having the slightest idea of what any of the Bible says about anything. And they certainly mis-portray both Jesus and his disciples, but in particular Jesus.

The Hard Left and New Atheism commonly assert that Jesus was a socialist, and that the Church should be an arm of the communist party. This idea is a complete misreading of the Biblical text. Jesus, when he spoke about helping the poor or widows was not spouting socialist nonsense. He was directing his followers to share, personally and individually, because all morality takes place on a personal level, and none takes place on a social level.

The Bible is so capitalist about ownership that in the Old Testament, you could not actually buy land owned by a member of another family group. Any land you purchased from them had to be returned during the year of Jubilee, every 50 years. The only exception to this were purchases made for making sacrifices to God.

Further, the actual history of the early Church in the

book of Acts we are given the story of Anninias and Sapphira. They lied about giving all the money they received from selling a plot of land to the Church as they promised. The response was that they rightly owned the land before their promise, and the Church – as well as God - made absolutely no claim on the land. They were responsible only for fulfilling the vow they made concerning the money, not for giving the Church or state their property.

An important part of the rest of the New Testament is spent taking up an offering for the Church in Jerusalem. The rest of the people also sold everything they had and gave it to the Church to distribute. There was only one problem with this practice; the Church was never meant to be a government welfare agency. Soon enough, everyone was broke. So when Paul went on his next mission trip, he collected an offering for the Jerusalem Church so they could eat until they managed to get their affairs in order.

This is everything but a ringing endorsement of socialism. Yet the hard left will continue to spout their propaganda about it, because they believe in their power to tell the rest of us how to live. They believe we will accept the big lie if they tell them often enough. They have a contorted view of the Church and spiritual matters since they accept nothing beyond the physical world. Terms like the Kingdom of God means nothing to a carnalist.

People do not seem to think of Christianity in a correct manner much at all. It seems to me that we, as limited creatures and strapped to the short measure of time we get to exist, the subject of religion is not very well understood by most. We make two huge mistakes on the issue; one, we separate the physical from the spiritual and second, we limit heaven to some faraway place that is only imaginary. A simple explanation may clear up some of the misunderstandings.

So imagine that time and space are a ramp lit from a spotlight above it. Down the ramp is forward in time and across the ramp is the physical world. There is a collection area somewhere to the side of the ramp. Individual creatures appear on the ramp, then fall off the side into the collection area at the edge upon death. It does not matter what the collection area is, it all falls under the light of the spotlight. The entire ramp is lit by the spotlight, from corner to corner.

The spotlight itself is the Kingdom of God, from God the source. It is not some faraway place, because just like the creatures on the ramp are always under the spotlight, everything is always in the Kingdom both once alive and afterwards. There isn't anywhere not in the Kingdom, and that Kingdom that has meaning due to the source, not the table that reflects it. No matter what you do and no matter where you go, you will always be in the Kingdom.

So for a Christian, the idea of the "here and now" lacks some meaning, since the here and now are no different than anywhere or anytime else. One either lives like they are in the Kingdom or they do not. Accepting the Kingdom, through the sacrifice of Christ, is how one is connected to the Kingdom. But one cannot be "brought into" the Kingdom, since there is no other place it is possible to be.

When understood properly, it is not an either-or proposition. While here, one should feed the poor and comfort the old and orphan because this is what the King demands, and we are subjects. Also while we are here we should worship and pray, for we are already in the Kingdom under the King, and what changes in the future is type and location, not a spiriting away to a different place.

The places in the New and Old Testaments that talk about "heaven" make it clear that this is only the seat of God's power - the bulb in the spotlight. It is not a permanent location, it eventually located in Jerusalem in the New Earth at the End of Days according to the Book of Revelations. Right back to the garden we go. Right back to the new "here and now".

So any argument that Christianity is not interested in the here and now is false. We may not agree with the Hard Left about the parts of being here and now that matter, but those are differences of degree or type - even as large as they are. Just because a believer does not understand the nature of their religion does not make them a hypocrite. It makes them unaware, or untrained, or poorly educated by the Church. But it does not automatically make them a hypocrite. You would not say that to someone who did not remember how to work a math problem or could not remember who the third President of the United States was on a test.

Worse, the Hard Left has absolutely not a single clue how power is accumulated. It isn't just done at the barrel of a gun. There are constant eddies and flows and changes in how power is spread over a social group beyond just political struggle. Success also brings money as the market responds. Ideas gather capital in different places than previously and moves some of the social power around and spreads it wider.

Others organize and place pressure on the power structure to share and take their needs and views into account. Some govern or administer the state and both use small amounts of power and assign it to others, through mechanisms such as courts. And we live in a time when it is easier to see who is doing what in the public sphere, providing some ability for us all to provide oversight.

Power in the real world simply doesn't look like or work like the oppressor/oppressed dichotomy set up by the Soviet academics in America and their acolytes. They live in an imaginary world in which everything is wrong, and all of us must be shouted down and burned to the ground. They are blind to all of it-and their massively outsized egos most of all. It turns out one must be blind to oneself before one puts one's own eyes out on the sharp spikes of ideology. It is a shame so many are willing to do so.

CHAPTER NINE
THE GREAT GOD ROME

When the Roman Empire was young and expanding, it took an interesting tack about the religious beliefs of it's enemies.   Rather than convert the society they were conquering, they were themselves converted.   Either near the city walls or on a high place on the border where the other forces could see, they offered a special sacrifice to the gods. But the Roman sacrifices were special.

Long before they invaded, they would do everything they could to learn about the religion of their victim from those who interacted with the defenders. They could be traders or diplomats or herdsman looking for pasture. Through this process the Romans would learn as much about the enemies' religious practices as they could. So just before the first battle, before the eyes of the enemy troops, they would with all carefulness make a proper sacrifice to the gods - but not their gods, *your* gods.

This alone was often a disturbing act to the poor opposing forces. Against the best military units in the history of the world at that time, a prayer was often the only chance the other side had. And now those prayers were undone as surely as a B-grade actress loosening a cheap corset. If it were not for Carthage and General Hannibal Barca Rome would have had no challenger at all. The end result was Rome knew many different gods; they adopted the Greek Gods, changing their names and making up new fables about them. They even brought in the Egyptian gods to a lesser extent.

The Hard Left in America and the New Atheist movement are more like the Romans than the lonely scientist shut up in his lab. They have many great gods. Scientific principle, environmentalism, postmodernism, communism, and many more make up their pantheon. Yet just like the Romans, they are practical, and place one god far above the others. You may be frowned upon and scolded for blaspheming one of these minor gods, but it is our resistance to one particular god that makes them murderous. And it is the same god held up before the people 2,000 years ago in Rome.

When the Christians first began to spread beyond the Judean cradle that made up its birthplace, they ran into bloody resistance from the Roman society. Because among the Romans, there was one practice that could not be rejected; Caesar. Every Roman was expected to toss a small pinch of powder into the flame of a candle, and when it went "poof" proclaim, "Caesar is Lord".

Never mind that by the time of Christ two Caesars had already sat on the throne of Rome, and they died just as all men die, as would all future emperors. But for the Romans, this was not mainly an act of person worship. Rather, it was a statement of solidarity and unity under Roman leadership. You were not actually claiming Caesar was Lord; you were proclaiming that Rome was Lord. It was an act of loyalty, a confession that the only good in humanity emanated not from any god at all, but from the men that ran the senate and led the troops into battle.

Romans may have flirted with, and even loved other gods such as Bacchus, the god of wine. But real power came not from the clouds or far away heaven but from Rome, the city of power. Even the legendary Roman belief in rule of law held only a distant secondary place to Rome. Rome, and all it represented was the true first love of all Romans.

It is the same for the Hard Left of America and the world today. Only they are more direct and less sly than their Roman forbears, for they demand we toss a pinch of powder into the candle flame and when it goes "poof" intone the all-important confession "Government is Lord". Blasphemy of government is the one sin for which they will not forgive. Just like the Romans, they use our separateness as an excuse to call us agnostic, to make the wildest claims against us as barbarians, to persecute us and blame us for every calamity that befalls mankind, both human and natural.

They are just like their Roman forefathers, and they hate us now with the same passion those ancients hated the early Church. And when they finally manage to incite and gaslight and propagandize the average citizen to give them power, they will be far bloodier towards us than the Romans were in times past. Make no mistake about it; the day the Hard Left truly comes to power the end will arrive for all those who will not bend knee to the modern Rome.

Government is the great god of the Hard Left; Bureaucros is his name, and he is the most powerful of all gods. He has the power to expand government reach and corrupt freedom. Some other gods, such as Kronos are also respected but not nearly as much. Kronos must depend on the poor aim of quasars to destroy his enemies, or hurl a stone at us in attempt to wipe us out from the reaches of the universe. 70 million years ago, Kronos wiped out the dinosaurs but that was a mere lucky shot, a one in a billion event that will not likely be replicated in another 100 million years.

Bureaucros is much more powerful, at least in the here and now; at a mere whisper tomorrow he may cause the deaths of a million men. Rather than a distant, cold ruler, he is in the here and now, and command men commit the most horrible and craven atrocities far beyond the mere imagination of average humans. It is he behind all the sacrificial gods of mankind that demand the murder of our children and our beating hearts be torn from our chest.

In return, he gives his followers drafty apartments and their daily crusts of bread, unless he is angry and leaves you to dig in the trash for your dinner. Bureaucros giveth, but he taketh far, far more away. He is a hard ruler, and impossible to please, as he demands the food from your table as well as his own.

And the Hard Left and New Atheists worship him wholeheartedly. Even anarchists are at heart slaves to Bureaucros and his demands. Along with him is his mistress Chaos, who sows destruction and famine and violence, salting the ground everywhere her foot has trod. He comes but to kill, steal, and destroy, through men his servants who find power and perverted pleasure in the blaming of others for their failure, and seeking revenge.

Bureaucros promises to level the playing field, to strip the powerful of their comfort and the corrupt of their gains. But his promises are empty, as he comes to devour every table and humiliate every man, the mighty for his pride and the humble for his greed. He must be resisted at all costs, and there is not enough blood in the whole world to pour out in the name of his resistance.

For the Hard Left and the New Atheists, the issue of being in control is paramount. Lack of government control is unacceptable. Every Hard Left answer involves bureaucrats taking control of social activities in order to manipulate society or nature. The only real value of the Hard Left is ease, to be brought about by the continual evolution of humanity and technology. I do not see serious evidence the Hard Left believes that people will eventually live forever, at least for long enough or soon enough to impact their behavior. They do seem to have accepted that death is inevitable. In the meantime they are only and solely interested in how difficult their lives are in the present world. Easing the human condition for themselves is the most powerful drive of the left. They live only in the moment and lack the patience to look more than a few weeks into the future. Everything is an emergency and must be fully corrected now, today, this very moment.

But how good are we at finding solutions to our problems? Hunger and poverty continue, both within society and internationally. Violence continues to be a problem, especially the militant violence of Islam. But even on smaller levels, issues remain unfixed. Drug and alcohol abuse and suicide continue unabated, and indeed seem worse than ever in the West. We still live under the grey skies of limitation and weakness. Divorce rips the fabric of family and society, damaging the framework of political and social cooperation.

Worse, the Hard Left does not have an answer for these issues. All of them have existed in whole at least since I was young. There were bombings by Jihadists in the 1980's. True, war on a large scale has abated, because societies around the world have made some economic progress, which requires violent behavior be smothered. So in many places, open warfare has become less common. But the asymmetrical warfare of Muslim extremists continues, and no actual answers to the other issues exist. Not even suggestions in most cases.

Since drugs are horribly destructive to individuals and families, the correct answer is to legalize them, so they are no longer a problem, but a source of taxes. However, one cannot honestly say America became a better place when prohibition was repealed. Drugs and alcohol are incredibly damaging to people and society. Yet they remain a shadow in our existence we cannot ever seem to successfully grapple with individually much less wrestle into submission socially.

But victory can only be found in submission. The answers lie somewhere other than in the papers and shallow mind tricks of those in academia. Think about it; the only way to eliminate the damage of drugs in society is to get everyone - literally everyone - not only to agree that drugs are bad, but to self-patrol so that no one actually uses them anymore. When you have people willing to use, then you end up where we are; a group of users that society patrols in order to attempt to manage the flow of product. Those are really the only two options available.

But there is literally no way to get the 300 million plus people in America to agree not to do drugs, and have them all live up to it from now on. Why? Because there are people who are not capable of understanding drugs are bad, and there are many, many more who are selfish enough that if they want to do drugs, that is what they are going to do. There are others that are rebellious and resist the outside messaging of others. Why do people commit adultery? Why do they embezzle money? Why do they shoot up schools?

Because they want to.

Until we come to recognize that reality, that the ills of society exist only because members of our society want them to, can we start to work on finding an answer, challenging people so that they don't want to do that any more. It is a difficult task, which is demonstrated in the campaign to end smoking cigarettes in America. The effects of cigarette smoking have been the leading cause of death in America, so there has been a sustained public effort to persuade people to not smoke for several decades.

According to the CDC, this public campaign against smoking has been moderately successful, as the percentage of Americans who smoke has fallen from 20.9% in 2005 to 15.5% in 2016. That is a sizable decrease, but it still leaves 37.8 million smokers who have not given up the practice. And that number may not go down much more, as 13.1% of adults aged 18 to 24 are smokers(1). There is clearly a disconnect for a sizable segment of society that are difficult to reach through education and social pressure. Even if they agree with the public message that smoking is bad for the health, they still may not be strong enough or motivated enough to stop.

That is where things can get crazy. We could go the way of the Philippines, and hire locals to kill smokers and their dealers to try to stem the flood. We could round them up and put them in gulags, but then we become a police state spying on each other. And even with all that, we probably will not ever eliminate the problem altogether. During the worst of the Soviet Union, you could still buy American jeans on the black market, and you can buy a

CD of rap music today in Mecca.

Markets are a lot like a squishy ball in that you can apply enough pressure to squeeze most of the interchanges down, but you will never totally get rid of it and the moment you let up it will bounce right back. And the West is uncomfortable with using these tactics and strategies as they know once government obtains real power over people that power is tempting and regularly misused. Unable to deter demand or eliminate supply completely, we do the compromise and put as much weight on the market for illicit drugs as we can, without eliminating the distance between the citizen and the government completely.

It may be possible one day that we will be able to reorder the brains of users so they will not desire those products, but who would trust the government with that power? If the government can make you not want cigarettes, they might be able to make you agree we should have a Supreme Ruler for Life, and I would suggest to you this would be a bad thing. Maybe eventually we will find some genetic markers for tendency to be addictive, but then again the possibility would be there for a prenatal inoculation that would make them immune to addictive behavior…and docile personalities the government can control.

We could open quite a can of worms, we have done it before. Here in the real world, there are no easy answers between our rights and our responsibilities to the people and society in which we exercise them. But there is one thing I can say definitively; eliminating traditional morality has weakened rather than strengthened the ability of the nation to create and maintain order within society. Has it collapsed completely? No, but around the edges there is a considerable amount of rot setting in that can devour resources and hamstring the effective use of our time and energy. Even in the worst national emergency addicts make poor soldiers or rescuers.

It is these kind of conundrums for which the Hard Left has no answers. They only seem to wish to walk this tightrope between anarchy on one side and Borg assimilation on the other, fully expecting the Borg to win out some day. This hardly looks like a wonderful bright future we are promised by the Hard Left, if only we would all become a part of their current hive mind. Just ignore the cyborg behind the curtain.

If we were wise then, we would return to the values of our ancestors, and once again order society so that it is politically and socially acceptable to stand up for real, meaningful values. But those values must come before Rome. Rome must serve them and us, rather than the other way around. But for that to happen, we must fight like our lives are at stake, as they are, since those who worship Rome will not let go of their idols willingly.

1.
https://www.cdc.gov/tobacco/data_statistics/fact_sheets/adult_data/cig_smoking/index.htm

CHAPTER TEN
LYING LIARS WHO LIE ALL THE TIME

The lies. The constant lying of the Hard Left bothers me more than anything else. And the lies are so deceptive; if you look at any claim of the modern Hard Left there isn't any truth at all in their propositions. Let's take a look at the economic history of the United States from the beginning of the 20th century until now to fully illustrate this constant misrepresentation of facts.

The first-wave leftism unleashed by Marx and his allies actually had a limited effect on the West. Europe and America did not become rich and powerful by having a controlled, top-down system of governance. For better or worse, most governance was left to the local populations. There were times when this worked like a charm. It took America a ridiculously short amount of time to settle the entire continent once the United Stated government gained possession of it. Texas didn't wait that long to claim it's freedom.

Of course, things went awry as well. Local control

allowed the evil of slavery to continue long beyond when it should have been ended, and it took a bloody and difficult war for the antislavery forces to make the practice end in the United States. The Wild West was an important if somewhat short period of time when American society lost most control over the frontier. It means that boors and cads like Custer can sometimes muscle their way to the top through sheer force of will and moxie. The British lost almost as many battles as it won for about the last 100 years of it's empire.

It lead to the Titanic, the Hindenburg, and hundreds of similar calamities. It led the conquering colonialists to mistake the cultural superiority that led to their power for racial and genetic prejudices. And it now too often leads my fellow conservatives to be knee-jerk reactionaries unable to adequate respond to and fight back against social decay.

But it also created the Golden Gate Bridge, the internet, and The Wonderful Wizard of Oz. It put a man on the moon and made civil right equality for black Americans all but inevitable. It defeated the Nazis in military battle and the original Soviets in a battle of ideology and economics. It has given us prosperity like the world has never known before, with half of the population of the entire world now being middle class. It's failures may be spectacular but so have people like Edison and Lincoln and Patton and Martin Luther King Jr. been.

This is not the story of the Hard Left. They see all people as being basically indentured servants both before and after the creation of the labor movement, except those who were lucky enough to get to belong to a union. Some good things came out of that movement, such as improved working conditions. Other not so wonderful effects occurred, such as the nearly total corruption of the union leadership starting in the 1950's.

The labor movement was able to be successful because there was limited amounts of labor available. Blacks were discriminated against and locked out of the best jobs and companies, often by the very people pushing for more power for laborers. And women were locked out of most jobs, both from the necessity to raise children and the physical fact there was much heavy labor work they could not do overall.

Starting in the 1950's this began to change quickly. Within a couple of decades, discrimination would be illegal, and women would slowly start having increasing access to the job market. So the American economy in a short amount to time managed to absorb an incredible number of extra workers. For a time, this caused wages to stagnate and helped cause high inflation, but the Reagan economic policies ended this for a 25-year streak of economic growth from 1982 to 2007.

But this was not the only drag placed on the American economy. Since 1980, the population of America has increased by 1/3 as well, as immigrants both legal and illegal poured into the country. America literally created more jobs in the decades following 1950 than we had in 1950. This did, however, have one negative effect; wage stagnation was the natural mathematical outcome of bringing this huge flood of warm bodies into the job market. For much of the last 6 or 7 decades labor shortages have been nothing more than a distant dream.

In a less dynamic economy, such expansion of the workforce would undercut wage growth completely and still leave pockets of poverty, just as we see in Europe today. These facts are not a part of the economic story of the Hard Left. They will tell you the opposite.

Lacking economic understanding and the ability to do simple math, the Hard Left places the blame of limited wage growth to the economic policies of conservatives rather than on labor growth where it belongs. They see the collapse of union power and prestige as due to the assault by conservatives and not caused by the very real forces of international competition and the replacement of manual labor with automation. For a few industries that still require heavy and dangerous work such as bricklayer and utility worker unions still exist.

But we don't need a website builder's union. Websites are difficult and require specialized skills that make competition for quality labor its own force when it comes to benefits and wages. The number of auto workers has shrunk to a small percentage of what it was in 1955, but other industries have blossomed and replaced those jobs. They're just different, that's all.

Our current issue politically is that we now have a generation of Americans who have experienced none of this, and only have the Soviet mutterings of their communist professors to go by. This is why I suggest you listen to voices like Jordan Peterson and others, crabby old men who are willing to tell you the truth that all that left wing propaganda is hallucinogenic poppycock. You will not end up in the worker's paradise promised by the Hard Left; you will end up in the gulag for not being sufficiently revolutionary like your also-unreasonably gullible forefathers did.

The rise of the Hard Left and their Brown Shirt army called Antifa ought to terrify any reasonable person. Not only is the current generation of Americans taught the same Soviet lies, they are taught the same failed Soviet response: blow it up. Burn it down. Breach the walls and level the village in order to rebuild it in the proper Soviet way.

Should they succeed, America will literally become the new Soviet Union, and will inherit all the weaknesses we see in the modern version of communism operating in China. America has become far less free over the last 50 years, and any remaining vestiges of freedom will be gone in the wind, most likely to never return in a meaningful way.

It will also be bloody, as all such enterprises are. Millions will die, and there will be a civil war that will make the last one look like a picnic should there be enough conservative forces left to enforce their independence. The economy will at least partially collapse, leaving millions more in abject poverty for the first time in their lives. And just as America is at it's weakest point, Islam will be at it's strongest in centuries.

The whole world will be on the verge of collapse into a second dark age that could last for millennia. All the gains we have made will be forgotten, wiped out through fatwa and intentional destruction. And here's he worst part; it will be our fault, individually, name by name. The guilty parties for the fall of the West can be literally named - you and me. This is the dark, dead-end alley your communist professors are leading you down. Your family and friends will die and be enslaved, and you will personally be to blame.

Yes, I know the Hard Left points to Europe and in particular the Nordic nations as being "wealthy" from socialism. This is also a lie. Here is what they don't tell you; the vast majority of this "wealth" is locked up in antiquities, paintings and sculptures and crown jewels and statues and archaeological buildings such as the Sistine

Chapel. This "wealth" is not easily fungible, and Europe produces neither more to replace it nor hardly any other advanced products to generate free cash flow. Europe has overall restricted business activity so much that after nearly 25 years of internet capability they have yet to produce a single major internet or IT company.

For this reason, most of Europe actually has much lower income than in America. There are some localized exceptions such as Switzerland which has a concentration of financial services. In the rest of the continent, such pockets of prosperity are extremely localized even in the "advanced" economies of Britain and France and Germany. London is rich, but not the rest of the country. In France, prosperity no longer even reaches into all the suburbs. And despite a quarter-century of reunification the old East Germany outside of Berlin has still not caught up with the rest of the country.

The rest of Europe is in even worse shape; Greece is a dumpster fire, and Italy not far behind. Portugal and Spain are unimportant backwaters, and the states that made up the old Yugoslavia are best known for recent war crimes. Old Soviet Block countries such as Poland and Hungary find themselves more bullied by than integrated into the EU. And bizarrely enough, they are also the only countries on the continent willing to be honest and stand up for traditional western values. Even more bizarrely, Americans consider them semi-fascists.

The world has gone crazy, and will take you down with it if you decide to listen to these voices of delusion. Inoculate yourself by learning the truth and standing up for it. It is the only hope the world has. Reject all versions of Anti-Semitism regardless of source. Understand this; the principles that have gotten us to this advanced place in society are the only ones that can keep us here. They are the only hope the rest of the world has as well, and we are incredibly late to start becoming evangelists for these western values.

This is the truth, all of it, no matter how angrily your communist professor desires to deny it. Mock and scorn them to frustration and shame, or one day in the future you will be far more despised for your willingness to allow all humanity to undergo tremendous suffering over a fantasy.

Here is the other truth about doing good; for those with foresight, the very direction of humanity's future may lie in our corporate hands. That one slight chance to truly move the needle of the world no matter how small should be enough to encourage us to the ultimate effort and sacrifice. That is how you join the ranks of those who fought at Tours and Hastings and Normandy. It cost many of them all.

If you wish to be a hero like that, let this battle cost you just as much. Refuse to accept going lower. Go higher. it's the right way to go.

RESPONSE

CHAPTER ELEVEN
THE STRUGGLE

You, the individual person reading this book, are the first answer to every problem humanity faces. The very first answer. Because what you personally do does matter. It matters more than you could ever imagine. There is one way in which your choices clearly make a difference; future potential. Our future potential is critical to all those who will live in the world we will leave them. Let me explain.

A lot - way too much in a way - of the people we see throughout history are those who have had an oversize impact on human civilization. This happens in two important ways; environment and genetics. Through these two mechanisms we can see the cumulative effects of human effort in general and specific ways.

Environmentally, it is an easy explanation. There is a reason the banking capital of Europe is Geneva and not Sarajevo. The two places have radically different histories, and those histories provide or deny the capability of civilizational development.   Geneva was a peaceful, generally free area where people could pursue commerce and wealth without undue difficulty long before the region of the Balkans found itself mired in armed conflict - some of it not all that long ago.

As the true intersection between western and eastern Europe and the path of invasion for Islam, the Serbs and their neighbors had to war and fight and build castles long after western Europe started looking outward at the rest of the world.   Think about this; the last major attempt at conquering Europe by the Muslims took place at the Battle of Vienna in 1683.   They were defeated by King Leopold of the Holy Roman Empire and his allies.

Think about that date for a second - Vienna was attacked by Turkish invaders and beaten back by the dark-age state of the Holy Roman Empire a mere 93 years before the Declaration of Independence.   And this was the third attempt at conquering Vienna since 1485.   The civilization you create, or manage to fight for is exactly the one you leave to the next generation.   And it will have no more potential than your effort gives it for very long periods of time.

Maybe if the Western leaders had taken the first invasion as seriously as they should have, they could have cut off access to Europe to the Muslims by about 1500. But a whole bunch of people in western and central Europe, including the British who were far away basically did little to nothing as a response to Vienna being attacked, made through choice/lack of choice by all the available parties to ignore the danger.

And so the poor Serbs and their neighbors still suffer today, more ignored by their so-called neighbors than ever even as over 500 years of history is ignored, and will spend the next few decades watching as Bosnia and Macedonia slowly become majority Muslim. This all matters. It's not just what Belgrade is today, but how every choice or action made or not made by all those who had an interest did or did not take made Belgrade what it is today.

We all then have a responsibility to look at what is going on in the world and respond. The caveat is that we have to be strategic and intelligent and honest enough to motivate us to do the right thing not just things that make us feel morally superior. Then we have to do it, regardless of the cost and suffering.

The other part of the equation can be described by the Biblical genealogy of Jesus. There are some surprisingly unreligious people there, including the prostitute Rahab. All of these people were particular in some way, from Kings like David to commoners like you and me. But the stories of all those people were important. And they participated in life, to the best of their ability, and that led through the generations to Jesus.

The same thing applies to every family. What difference would it have made if Hitler's father had been a successful businessman? Or maybe an aristocrat? So much of what makes every person who they are is directly ingested through the values and beliefs and attitudes of the people they are raised among. How different would Gandhi have been if he had been born Japanese? How about India?

And what would Einstein have been like if he had been born to a different father? How about a different mother? Would he still have been a genius? Would he have been born with down's syndrome? In the long run, all of our decisions work on a macro level, but on a micro level, there are things that you have influence on that no one else does.

Let me share with you a story about a man in the middle of a forest in the middle of the winter in Belgium in 1944 if I may. He was part of the Battle of the Bulge, some of the men who were thrown into the battle as a stopgap to slow the German drive until Patton could arrive.

The Germans were desperate to find new weapons to help win the war, and this man was going to become the victim of one of them. German bombs and shells often contained small incendiary pieces with phosphorus or a semi-solid flammable material similar to crude napalm. While in the field, this soldier had a shell of some sort explode in the trees behind him – a common occurrence, as the trees themselves would fall and splinter, sending shards of wood and tree tops crashing into the American positions. This solider was hit in the middle of the back by one of the incendiary pieces from the ordinance.

Fortunately, this young soldier had made friends as the Americans crossed France towards the Reich. He was wearing a heavy winter coat over a jacket over another warm top, then a thermal undershirt. This young soldier managed to get all that off just in time to have the piece of incendiary material fall harmlessly to the ground. Only one more layer of clothing, an everyday tee shirt lay between him and death.

I happen to know about this man because he was my grandfather, Winfield Cullum. He literally survived the Battle of the Bulge by stripping. He was lucky. And that began a series of events that literally led to me. Later in the spring, they wanted to promote him to sergeant, but he did not want to be responsible for ordering men to their deaths.

So he got drunk one evening and punched out an officer in the middle of a crowded bar, a crime he could not later deny. After a short stint in the brig, they sent him home instead of keeping him as part of the occupation forces, so coming home was his second important act. It was a good thing, too.

Back in Portsmouth, Ohio, a young woman named Delena was working at a decent job for Mitchellace, a nationally respected manufacturer of shoestrings. She was a recently divorced mother of a little girl named Dianna. Delena's first husband turned out to be abusive, so she chose to accept the stigma at the time and divorce him. Dianna was my mom. I never met nor knew him, my mom's biological father.

Having a daughter to raise and a home to run, Delena was not really interested in dating. It was only my grandfather's patient insistence that finally wore my grandmother down and got her to yes. They didn't really hit it off at first – their first date was to a bar, and it lasted about five minutes – and those facts were collected from her, not him.

But it did click, and when it did they became inseparable. She was his best fishing buddy. Many years later, when I was a young teen, a younger woman tried to lure him away from her. I know this because he told us all about it and laughed. I doubt it ever occurred to him to consider it much less take the woman up on it.

It was a good thing they fell for each other, too. When they married, he moved them out of Portsmouth, several miles away to far end of the little town west of the Scioto River called West Portsmouth. They bought a house on a road called Carey's Run, just a mile or so from the boundary of Shawnee State Forest. He loved to hunt rabbits and squirrels and raccoons, and wanted to be able to go without driving all day and being too far from home.

Diana now had to switch schools, make new friends and settle in among a different group of people than when she lived in Portsmouth. It was through that new group of people she met my father. Ergo, me.

Without that soldier undressing in the forest and saving his own life, I probably would not be here today, and this book would not have been written, and my thoughts unshared. My newly divorced grandmother probably would not have dated much less married anyone else for several years. And since there were a lot more houses in Portsmouth than West Portsmouth it is unlikely they would have moved so far away. So there was a very high likelihood my mom would have married someone else, and they would have had different children.

I am who I am because of all these people, and their stories and all the things they taught me, good or bad. There is so much of our lives that is a coin flip, often without our knowledge or even existence such as in my case. It is so incredibly that we share and learn and know these stories and pass them on like I am doing now.

Every day, some boy somewhere through his father starts to get the picture of what it is to be a man. Ditto for girls. Yes, interaction with even family members can be frustration and heartbreak, but you never know what discussion will break the dam open, what advice may click that light on in someone's mind that motivates them to repair a relationship or ask forgiveness for a wrong they have done or have a change of heart.

That is not to say you should argue with someone just to make sure you make your point. That's crazy, and rarely productive. I block people on social media, because I am not out to argue, merely to say what I want and feel compelled to say. As someone who is speaking intentionally to the public I do not intend to argue with 7.6 billion people. I expect for those who do read my words and consider if I am speaking truth or not. I am not interested in debate per se, though that depends on the circumstances.

No, in life you do your best for both public good and the good of those personal to you. This is your charge in society. Look around, and you can find thousands of examples of people creating real hope in other people's lives. Paradise California was ravaged by the fires of November 2018, but the girl's volleyball team wanted to play their next volleyball game like normal - even though they had lost everything including uniforms. They felt it was important to give their neighbors something to cheer for and a little distraction from their losses.

Their opponent, Forest Lake Christian School used the game as a fundraiser, providing new uniforms and equipment and $300 for each student. That is the kind of thing you can do, even if all you did was give the people collecting the entrance fees $10 instead of $5. Only your specific part is little but joined with others it is big.

https://usatodayhss.com/2018/calif-hs-volleyball-program-rallies-to-support-team-town-reeling-from-wildfires

This, my friends, is how life is done.

CHAPTER TWELVE
HOW TO BE CHANGE

I don't believe in you. No, really. Comfort brings corruption, and corruption is the fertile ground of collapse. And I know the average American is willing at least to be corrupt enough to purchase homes they could not afford by the millions in the vain hope of getting rich quick. And I know that a huge part of the American population will deny the dangers of Islamic radicalization, calling me worthless terms like "Islamophobe" - a charge both valueless and meaningless.

So when I say "know thyself", I am really talking about understanding and properly seeing the way modern western life has made all of us soft. Then, we need to repent - to turn away from that softness and change. We must change ourselves, our societies, and our future. We must admit that we have lacked the courage and conviction of our forefathers to do what is necessary, to take the bullet for others if need be so that our people can continue and thrive and prosper.

We must also recognize our place in time and history. We are entering a period of time where the entire future of humanity hangs in the balance. Mankind has been here before, and it is up to us to decide whether we will likewise rise to the occasion. Society is a funny thing; we lift our voices before we lift our hands and act.

We need to speak the truth, that we are living in one of the most critical times in human history. Five times previously the enemies of freedom rose up to try and enslave us; during the first Muslim invasion ended at Tours, the second and third Muslim invasions ended at the battles for Vienna, and the Soviet and Nazi attempts at conquering the world.

By the turn of the 22nd century, Islam will have recovered from it's defeats to be the most powerful society on earth, well on it's way to dominating the world or it will not. That depends on us, whether we will steel ourselves, be willing to make the necessary sacrifices to build up our nations and our societies or not. It is simple, stark, and true.

Apologists will lie and say that Islam is just like Christianity was at first, it is just a few hundred years of development behind. But Christianity was always more peaceful than other religious beliefs in the West, even under the Roman Empire. And we don't have 600 years for them to catch up. Within the next seven decades they will have come to the point of having the power to expand by force, which they *will* use.

Yes I am trying to light a fire under your behind. Your grandchildren will suffer the consequences of what you choose today. Our economic mismanagement is a huge issue, that is true, but it pales in comparison to living in an Islamic state. That is the current end game of our modern world, and the direction history is actually bending in.

Being raised in free nations, we shine off definitive statements by claiming we are going to "agree to disagree", but this is a luxury we can no longer afford. That is not what the Muslims are doing - they are reproducing faster that we are not just in Tehran, but in Berlin and Paris and Stockholm as well.

I will again say we need to repent, and confess we can no longer afford to navel-gaze our way into our preferred psychosis, that we need to have clear minds and strong hearts if we are going to continue our way of life. No longer can we afford a huge population of weird and emotionally twisted people to shine off their responsibilities to the few of us willing to join the military and have children and be greedy capitalists. These are leeches that criticize the people they hide from the world behind, and we need to understand they are not ethical nor oppressed and call them out on their nonsense.

We must admit the power of doing good, not for "persecuted" groups but for our families and our societies and our nations in specific. We need competing values with which to combat and reject the political specter of Islam just as we did communism and national socialism. We need our confidence back, to put the history of our nations in the proper light so we can focus not on the past but the future. Yes, there was much about the past that was evil and violent all around the world. We can recognize that without allowing it to cripple us.

I will say it since so few others will; we have done more good over history than evil, or we would all still be living in mud huts. We deserve to receive not just blame for the bad but honor for the good we have provided to the world. We in the West do not deserve to suffer for our past sins, which are no worse than others. We do not deserve to be forced to pay restitution any more than any other people.

We and our culture do not deserve to be destroyed. We deserve to be celebrated and honored in every nation that has electricity or proper homes or any measure of freedom, all of which was developed by the historical movement so many despise. But it all begins with you and your family. It's not that we do not deserve defeat, it is that you personally do not deserve destruction, regardless of your skin color or past culture or beliefs.

Your kids do not deserve to be left behind because they are white, or Jewish, or Asian. We do not deserve public denouncement for who we are and how we live. We are all the lucky ones, to be born and live in the cradle of freedom, for which we should feel gratitude and a deep sense of being blessed. And we can take pleasure in the way we improve the living conditions of the whole world, if just by adoption. Just the fact that the Islamic Republic has to block internet services ought to persuade us of the power of doing good.

Doing good is a legitimate sacrifice, to God and society and home alike. There is nothing wrong with being normal, or happy or successful. Those things are our heritage, one that we are beginning to share with the rest of the world, and I for one would have it no other way. Did you know that as of this year every single village in India has electricity according to the humanprogress.org web site?

https://www.moneycontrol.com/news/india/after-over-70-years-of-independence-india-completes-electrification-of-all-of-its-villages-2559727.html

If your children are to survive, it is time to rethink our coddling of the dysfunctional. I do not want to see anyone abused, but there is no reason to listen to their incessant croaking as if it were gospel truth. Most of the work of modern academia and the beliefs of their acolytes are based on nonsense and emotional dysfunction. We need to tell the truth that they are creepy, and a lot more than a little nasty. We must demand a certain amount of civility and honesty from our public voices and we should denounce those who fan the flames of emotionalism for political gain.

We must repent of seeing our culture as more corrupt than others. Western culture is far superior in some ways, and probably not as good in others. We should stand as first among equals then, appreciating the other civilizations of the world while not denying the value of our own. Outside Islamic nations, much of the world lives in mixed cultures anyway, blending in some parts of Western influence with their own traditional society. There is nothing wrong with this, and it just proves the strength of all our countries' ability to adapt despite the despicable attacks of our enemies.

Let's do it. Let's repent of this multicultural nonsense, and instead build a foundation for a truly better future for all of us. Repent of what is in your own heart, the grimy residue of whatever parts of postmodernism you have absorbed as your own. Throw off the hollow propaganda of those who wish revenge on you for the accident of your birth and who wish to destroy your children.

Repent, and let it go. And let all of us get back to the important work of life.

It is the only way.

CHAPTER THIRTEEN
THE REIGN OF PEACE

There is one thing that hardly anyone mentions, but I have come to value more than anything else; peace. There are different kinds of peace, some more valuable than others. Peace between nations has great value, and has been the underlying principle that has made our modern prosperity possible. Military conflict both destroys structure and infrastructure but impedes the ability of people to work and produce.

What is lacking in modern life is internal peace that exists in the heart of the person. Part of the issue is materialism points only to the raw objects that make up our world, and that overemphasis leaves us without a reasonable foundation for internal peace. Having things is nice, I have a few things myself, but consumerism is shallow and incapable of providing true inspiration much less peace.

So people look in other places for generating self-satisfaction, namely activity and experiences. These are also inadequate, because to a lesser degree they share the selfishness of impulsion with consumerism. They still mis-value the person - you - that is the agent behind any activity. This is a critical distinction, because correct self value creates a healthy inner life of peace.

True self value cannot be based on activity, as people engage in acts that are both good and evil. At best, we can create a hierarchy in which we separate good and evil acts and even order them from worst to best. This is still inadequate as on a daily basis I probably do a couple bad things - even on my very best days. And so do you.

And while it is OK and even good to take credit and even pleasure in doing good, which I encourage by the way, when those acts are used to measure human good, they often become a warping influence on the ego causing self-pride and lowering the value of others. The truth is most of humanity is much the same in situation, rather middling about good and evil with some people such as Abraham Lincoln and Martin Luther King rising to the occasion of the crisis they face.

Most of the rest of us will do good and evil on a more universal level. Just as we do not forget those who sacrificed themselves in the great military conflicts in our history, so most of us do our most good in our own organized activities. While we may not be remembered by name as are many of those who died for country and principle in the past are unknown we still get to share in that corporate level of good.

Experiences cannot be a transport to peace of mind as experiences can only be had as a consumer. And while experiences can teach and we can certainly learn from our interactions with the world, they do not of themselves have the capability of creating peace. No experience can create value unless we bring it to opportunity through activity - so we're thrown back on mere actions again.

Since consumerism, activity, and experience cannot help us have peace, we must look elsewhere. But where will we look then for peace? In truth. There are two things that will lead us to peace if we will but be honest about ourselves. I believe that good can win if we understand our agency in being the only creatures capable of intentionally doing good. And that brings a measure of peace.

The other part lies in accepting our smallness. Knowing no one person can do enough to fix the world unless you happen to walk on water, and none of us do. We are small, and our power is limited. But this is good, because it limits our responsibility for doing good as well.

The Bible makes it clear that God decreed humans should die after the fall. This limits our ability to do good or evil, as we have limited time and energy to practice either. Our limited power is from the same place, and we should be able to see that strong concentrations of power can go to the evil just as it can to those who are good. Our ineffectualness is strategic mercy given by the creator.

Even if I take an entire day (and I have) and I do nothing but play around on the internet and act a bum, God loves me no less than on those days when I do spectacular good. Our creator takes into consideration my smallness as part of His deign as accepts it in me. I am valued because I carry His DNA and not just for my actions.

And even then, I still have potential. At any moment I can write as I am doing right now or choose to do any of a dozen good things. I have both potential and imprint, even though I am only a small piece of the universe. Peace comes from knowing that I am connected to the spiritual as a part of life itself.

But it goes even deeper than that, as I believe there is a power in the universe that does indeed bend the arc of history towards good. I live as a part of that spiritual river, and my acceptance of that reality brings peace. Yes, I am being somewhat obtuse, because I do not intend on being the finisher of anyone's faith. This is merely a guide to get you started in the right direction, to see the first few steps.

After that, I leave you to choose your spiritual path. I would only leave you with directions; I chose my own faith based on two criteria. First, that if there is a creator, we were created as an act of love (though it may not seem like it), so He must express that love. Second, any creator that brought us forward out of love would not abandon us, but is willing to interact with those beings He loves so. Use that criteria, and I think you will choose wisely as well.

In this there is peace, as I know I am loved in the universe that seems so cold. With real peace in my heart, doing good becomes less an act to gain approval, but rather a response to the fact I am loved. That is the difference between the faithful and the atheist; there is no one to truly love the unbeliever, as we frail humans are inadequate to the task. If you think human love is enough to live on, you will be horribly disappointed.

Here lies a freedom no other philosophy can offer you; by understanding and accepting the love of a creator, we are free to not worry. There is no question of doing good or bad; we can celebrate good and repent of evil. We can be fearless, for salvation can be lost, but not because of any specific action. Any act can be forgiven if we ask, as long as we choose to do so.

Instead of focusing on whether I have done enough good, I can focus on what good I can do right from where I am. No pressure, no unrealistic expectations. Those who we look up to can be a model for us to follow rather than an artificial measure to live up to. We can rejoice in the success of others without diminishing ourselves. We are the trophies of our maker, and our good works are extras, jewels set in our record to shine there forever.

We do not have to give up right judgment either. Bad people can still be spurned, and if they need to be, punished for their crimes. But after this, they can be forgiven and given another chance. The goal is to bring along and encourage everyone to willingly doing good, that is how a good society is created. We must value doing good above all other activities. But it must be voluntary, it cannot be forced.

If you find peace separate from your specific place in the world I believe you will find it to be the greatest gift you can give yourself. It will set you free like nothing else can. Peace of heart is the most valuable thing you can gain, and the best part is; it's totally free.

It costs nothing to believe in a God who loves you. Nothing at all. All you have to do is accept it as true. The rest is up to you. But let me add another layer to this beyond that step - doing good can be fun. Imagine what it would be to sit at a cafe and listen to the conversation between J.R.R. Tolkien and C.S. Lewis. Imagine what it would be like to (fill in the blank) that brings you joy and helps others. And maybe even causes you to learn.

Here's a gift for you; like I have so far, do not measure the value of your skills and activities based on the results you get. It may be that only your friends and family recognize your drawing skill, so let that be enough. You may or may not ever become a famous artist, but create it anyway, for if nothing else it enriches those around you, and that is enough value to be priceless. Have peace in your value and joy in those who share it with you and do not allow ambition to place a price tag on happiness. There is no such thing.

Like every gift, peace must be both given and received. The package left setting on the porch for a few years will eventually be ruined in the rain. So are the spiritual gifts we receive from our creator. Accept with gladness these gifts and allow them to change the content of your heart. I can promise you will never regret it.

The only rule is in order to have peace, you must be willing to be small-just the right size for what you really are. You are neither an insignificant speck of dust nor the mental Godzilla of the solar system, trampling nature under your feet. You are just a person, a small force capable of a long but limited number of tricks, living among other people just like you. You should neither rule nor grovel, but exercise your power to contribute, thus pass on your gifts to others.

When that is enough for you, your right-sizing of your ego will serve both you and others well. And in it, you will find the room for eternity in your heart, and peace will suddenly be available. Then you will be real, which is achieved when the size of your psyche matches the size of your physical imprint. Choose to learn peace.

It is well worth the practice.

CHAPTER FOURTEEN
SOME FINAL WORDS

When it comes to surface behavior humans are not particularly hard to program or reprogram. We know this, we have seen it in history and in behavioral psychology. But that is only superficial stuff, like smoking and fear of squids. We know what to do to adjust someone's behavior when it comes to phobias and other basic issues.

I was never quite afraid of heights when I was a child and teenager. I was at times uncomfortable. But I live in Arizona now. I've hiked the Grand Canyon and want to go back soon. I climb Camelback Mountain or Piestewa Peak regularly as I have come to love hiking. I got over being uncomfortable with heights pretty quickly. When I moved to Arizona permanently in 2001 I decided to quit smoking. So I slapped on a nicotine patch, hopped on a Greyhound bus to Phoenix and basically slept for three days. When I got off the bus, my habit was broken. I threw away most of a box of Nicorette gum, I only used three pieces and didn't really need them.

The problem is, the limits to cognitive therapy end when we get beyond these types of superficial behaviors. Emotional and perceptive processes are not nearly so easily adjusted. For those among us who are overoptimistic and never see nothing but blue skies, who are just so darned happy that they'll be damned if grandma dying is going to bring them down, there is little we can do to help. For those who are perpetually grey, living in a cloudy world where the kids are always sick and the car never runs right and the cat always has the sniffles, there is little we can do for you either.

Because we are dealing with interior and often emotional processes we lack the same type of cognitive control we do with mere habit. No one has a nice warm tub of happiness you can soak in like we can for those who have a fear of water. We can't introduce you little by little to joy the way we can those who fear spiders or snakes. And in a society that has some strange beliefs about the life of the mind there is little hope we will make much progress controlling these attributes anytime soon if ever. It is hard to convince people they need to change when all they hear from society is that they are perfect just the way they are. It is difficult to rule over your emotions and prejudices and the other dragons in your soul.

Emotions are often times necessary and good, but they were never meant to be the lodestar to our lives and future. We were meant to have emotions, but they are not all good. Like all else in the world they have been twisted in our weaknesses. Worse, we live in a society that places way too much emphasis on emotions and not enough on reasoning and logic. We feel too strongly and think too weakly and that is our failure.

When it comes to the truly hard work of creating your psychological world and grappling with the issues of your mind, you will find you are mostly on your own, and it is here that faith in a Creator can come in handy. The recesses of the mind are not like peninsulas drawn on a map. You need to see for yourself the necessity of your own change. And you need a guide to those internal worlds to help you untangle the complicated processes that cause you to misunderstand the world around you.

What you don't need is for society to encourage you in your iniquity. You don't need stories that motivate you in your deficiencies. You do not need praised for your imperfections. Instead, you need to be lovingly corrected, directed to look at the areas where you go off the rails, and why. Someone who can shine a spotlight on those hidden motivations and help you grapple with them successfully. In short, you need God. And others.

Modern society fails it's members not due to too little pride, but too much. Of all the things humans lack, self-esteem is not actually one of them. Since everyone is selfish by nature, even the depressed are evangelists for their views of the world. We say we are just sticking to the science, guided by facts, but that is only when those facts, the theories go our way. Otherwise we care not one whit for science or truth or anything else.

Yet humanity has only advanced in as much as we are adaptable to our surroundings, able to take proper measure of ourselves and the world we live in and respond correctly. We can still do that to a moderate measure when it comes to the hard sciences, but clearly our social constructs have not kept up. We are no nearer Utopia than we were when the book was written. So we are encouraged to abandon the few things we know are true about our fellow man in exchange for the fantasies of a perfect society.

Society cannot be better than the members who make it up and contribute to it. The real problem with postmodernism is that it does not change the nature of individuals, and there is no such thing as "social change". Social change is not a leading indicator of belief, it follows the beliefs already established in society.

So in a lot of ways, God is inevitable. And really, there are only two choices; organization through cooperation or at the end of a gun. We know how the end of a gun thing turns out, at least those of us with sense do. Cooperation and moderation are clearly better.

It is our lifestyle of ease that has us confounded. We were promised that ease and entertainment would bring us to the promised land of bliss. It turns out the more prosperous people are the unhappier they are. It also turns out that floating upon an endless ocean of entertainment merely sets us adrift in our own little dinghies of boredom.

So we look for an answer from the very frauds that brought us here. They now tell us that meaning will be found in our subjugation. Wasn't that the point all along? No matter how it is said, the promise is always the same; "Arbeit Macht Frei". Except it doesn't. It's not what we need. I'm not so sure it is even what we want.

What do we really want? I think that is the same as it has always been. We crave beauty, and meaning, and to have joy in ourselves to quiet the deep sensation of being inadequate.

How to obtain this? By doing good. By patrolling our own borders, by defending those things we get meaning from. By defending the story of our predecessors who brought us to this wonderful place in the face of tragedy. But mostly by giving the next generation a world we did not only live in and use for our gain, but that we improved and built up with our own hands.

Really, a legacy is all we will ever have. But should you find peace in all of this, you will find it enough. It is my earnest prayer you will consider where you are and who you are and what is to come. Then, by taking your small place in history, you too can be credited with doing enough.

And that is all that should ever be asked of you.

God bless,
Thomas Spriggs

ABOUT THE AUTHOR

Thomas Spriggs has lived in the Phoenix metro for an interminable number of years. He is an award-winning graduate of the Walter Cronkite School of Journalism. He is currently an explorer, apprentice musician and fan of Jordan Peterson.
And as always, delightfully crabby.

www.ingramcontent.com/pod-product-compliance
Lightning Source LLC
Chambersburg PA
CBHW031119250726
48655CB00004B/1767